THE ROBERTS COMMENTARY SERIES

AMOS

A Practical Commentary on the 30th Book of the Bible

Dr. Jeremy Roberts

AMOS: A Practical Commentary on the 30th Book of the Bible

PUBLISHED BY JEREMY ROBERTS MINISTRIES

Copyright © 2018 Dr. Jeremy Roberts

Cover Design by Colette Groves

ISBN-13: 978-1719183154

ISBN-10: 1719183155

CONTENTS

1 | A MESSAGE FROM GOD IN UNSETTLED TIMES

Amos 1:1–2

Amos 1:1–2 says, *[1] The words of Amos, who was among the shepherds of Tekoa, which he saw concerning Israel in the days of Uzziah king of Judah and in the days of Jeroboam the son of Joash, king of Israel, two years before the earthquake. [2] And he said: "The LORD roars from Zion and utters his voice from Jerusalem; the pastures of the shepherds mourn, and the top of Carmel withers."*

It is striking to note the first and last words of the first verse of this prophecy: "The words of Amos . . . two years before the earthquake." This is a prophetic word from God to be given during shaky, unsettled, earthquake times. An earthquake comes with unexpected suddenness and renders its victims absolutely helpless.

A few years ago, my family and I journeyed to Cross Church in northwest Arkansas where I preached. We were sitting on the couch in our hotel room, and all of a sudden, the walls began to shake. We were on the fifteenth floor of the Embassy Suites, and the floor began to shake. Could it be? An earthquake in Fayetteville, Arkansas? Yes, it was! It was a 4.7 magnitude earthquake that was centered a few miles away in northeast Oklahoma. Thankfully, we were safe. However, it really scared us. It was unexpected. Our daughter was crying. Had the furniture and pictures on the wall not been secure, things could have become dangerous and we would have been completely helpless.[i]

It is not without deeper significance that Amos' message precedes by two years an earthquake. Amos was God's kind of man during shaky and unexpected times. Politically, the foundations were already quivering. Beneath the substantial, substantive appearing life of the nation of Israel, economically, just around the corner, they're on the verge of fiscal and economic judgment.

Three decades after Amos spoke, in 721 B.C., when the ten tribes of Israel found themselves in ruination, out of the ashes and depression, they fought to find words that would interpret their experience.[ii] It was out of the book of Amos that the subsequent, disastrous generation came to know what it was to live in unsettled, shaky times.

Are things really so different 2800 years after Amos' message? Politically, have we not known what it is to have the ground quiver beneath our feet? Economically, do we not sense the fact that economic judgment or catastrophe is yawning at us like a gaping chasm? Just around some corner of the road. Is there no indication at all that our well-structured society might come unraveled? Just as Amos spoke to shaky times in *his* generation, he speaks to unsettled times in *our* generation.

What kind of man does God use to speak during unsettled times? Let's look for a moment at the man God uses during such a time as this. Amos 1:1 says, "The words of Amos . . . which he saw . . ." Now, we speak of *measuring* our words, but we seldom speak of *seeing* our words. But there was granted to Amos to have an insight which was molded into foresight so that in the history of his generation, Amos *saw* the Word of God. It is given to men who minister during earthquake times to see things that are not seen by the myopic multitude of their contemporaries.

Why did Amos *see* the Words of God in his generation? How may we *see* the Word of God inscribed into ours? Amos could see deeply because he saw from a place of quiet perspective. He was among the shepherds of Tekoa.[iii] This tiny village was on a rugged, rustic, running ridge ten miles south of Jerusalem.[iv] On a clear day, one could stand on the ridge that embraced Tekoa, and looking to the west he could see the azure waters of the Mediterranean Sea. It might be that to the north, he could see the capital city of Judah, the city of David.[v]

Now, King David had been dead for nearly two centuries.[vi] From the rugged ridge, he could look to the east down that deep, chasmic ascent of rugged brush and terrain all the way to the Dead Sea that glimmered in the heat waves. Tekoa was a place of unusual perspective and quiet reflection.

However, not everyone even in Tekoa could see what Amos saw. Evidently, we gather from the prophecy, he had never journeyed far from home. Somehow, because of his infrequent visits to the marketplaces in the capital city, because of snatches and bits of news from lands afar, as the sweeping gaze of Amos moved from the west, to the north, to the east. He saw the word of God as it was addressed to the multitudes in lands he had never visited.

Amos marched to the beat of a different drummer and saw things that others did not see. The man whom God uses to speak in any earthquake times is a man who will have a different, lonely perspective and will see things as his contemporaries do not see them.

As a disciple of Jesus Christ, you are under an obligation to have a radically different perspective to living in these days. The mindless, milling, multitudes will not see what the lonely Amos of the 21st Century will be able to see—that is the Word of God—in the history of our day. Tekoa was a lonely place, but the man who lived there saw what others could not see. The man who stands for God in shaky times when civilizations quiver and when the underpinnings are in the process of giving way must have that different and lonely perspective.

I. The Person God Uses in Unsettled Times (v. 1)

Amos 1:1 says, *The words of Amos, who was among the shepherds of Tekoa, which he saw concerning Israel in the days of Uzziah king of Judah and in the days of Jeroboam the son of Joash, king of Israel, two years before the earthquake.*

What about the person God uses in unsettled times? This man looks beyond his own narrow and confining responsibilities. Isn't it easy to just fulfill the responsibilities on your plate, then desire to go home and relax? Jesus asked us to go the extra mile, though (cf. Matt 5:41). Notice that Amos was among the shepherds of Tekoa. Further in the book, we learn that Amos was a keeper of an ugly, black-wooled, stumpy-legged, ill-born-faced sheep called the *Makah*. They were said to be ugly domestic beasts. And yet they were prized for their sleek and raven-colored wool.

We're told that the life of a shepherd is a hereditary life.[vii] From father to son, in Amos' family, the narrow, restricting, confining occupation of keeping the *Makah*—the ugly, ill-formed, stunted sheep had been passed from father, to son, to grandson. With such a perspective, Amos might have been like the common lot of men. He may have never looked higher than the scrub brush that grew around his feet in the slim breezing that was the pastureland of Tekoa.

Since Amos was willing to look up and risk his own responsibility, he ceased to protect sheep, and instead became the spiritual shepherd of an entire nation.

We can learn what it is to see the Word of God and to speak for the Word of God as we understand that any man who so does must lift himself up from the comfortable tasks in his home town and give himself to the madness of a mess of a world that is crying out the judgment of God. An encounter with Amos, and I've encountered him several times in this book, always leads me to a time of discomfort.

It raises me to ask the same question that Pierre Berton, a Canadian journalist asked: "Am I simply an occupant of the comfortable pew?"[viii] How often do we ignore God by staying enclosed in the narrow, confining, restricted orb of our immediate, mundane, and trivial responsibilities? Necessary though they may be, we never look up from the scrub brush at our feet and see the Word of God in our generation.

What kind of person does God use in unsettled times? God uses a person with a different, lonely perspective. God uses a person who looks up from the confines of immediate preoccupation and responsibility. But in another sense, He uses any person who will make himself available to be used by God.

Have you ever done a profile of the prophets? When you and I ask ourselves, ordained or unordained, laity or clergy, whatever we may call ourselves, "Can God use me?" Nothing is more salutary than for us to look at the prophets.

Isaiah

We find a man of aristocratic heritage like Isaiah. He always walked with confidence. When apprehended by the Lord, he said, "Here am I. Send me." He seemed to often walk with positive strength and accomplishment. He was a statesman in the midst of kings. He was a poet and a literary genius. And God used Isaiah.

Jeremiah

However, God also used Jeremiah. A man who was so timid and uncertain in the aftermath of God's apprehending him that he said "I am but a stammering youth" (Jer 5:15). He was a man who became depressed to the point of suicide so that he cried out "cursed be the man that brought the news of my birth" (Jer 20:15). He was a man who accused the very God who called him and promised Jeremiah he would be an unfailing stream of having become a delusive God who had held His prophet like a locust on the end of a string, jerking it just to see his wings fall.

Hosea

Also, God can use a Hosea. He was not a statesman like Isaiah, nor was he a pathological like Jeremiah. He was a man into whose very heart and home there came the brokenness that terrifies and the redemptive love that heals.

You and Me

I find a great deal of reluctance to really, internally, viscerally, at the innermost level believe that God could use me. But if He could use an Isaiah, if He could use a Jeremiah, if He could use a Hosea, and yes if He could use the keeper of ugly, stunted, ill-formed sheep, who had known nothing but the smallness of Tekoa, then surely He could use you and He can use me.

II. The Message God Brings in Unsettled Times (v. 2)

Amos 1:2 says, *"And he said: 'The LORD roars from Zion . . .'"*

That is the motto of this book. That is the overture to Amos' symphony. It is the preface to his message. "The Lord roars from Zion." Zion is the ideal city from God. "The Lord roars . . ." What did that mean and what could it mean?

It reflects the immediacy of irrevocable judgment. It is given to some men in some generations, "Brace yourselves! For judgment is coming." Amos, the man with insight and hence with foresight was a man who had to say to his generation repeatedly, "Brace yourselves! For judgment is coming."

Often, Amos sat on a moonless and starless night in the pasturelands of Tekoa and more than once he heard the fierce roar of the predatory lion, and he knew as a shepherd that when that roar had been sounded, the lion was already in the process of pouncing on a helpless member of the flock. You see, a lion does not roar accept just as he leaps into the moment of acquisition and judgment.

Word Study of *ROAR*

When Amos told his generation "The Lord roars from Zion," he was telling them, "Brace yourselves. For the intervention of God is already leaping into progress in this unjust generation." The burden of Amos' message is that Jehovah has roared. The significance of *Jehovah* should be taken in full—I will be what I will be—as that name perhaps means. "I am that I am" (Ex 3:13) and I will speak freely and spontaneously to every generation . . . even if it is of impending judgment. To compound the stark reality of this message, Amos says the Lord "utters His voice from Jerusalem." The Hebrew suggests thunder for that pastoral, desert people—thunder![ix] Its rumbling rarity is a mystery. It is a surprise. It is a threat. They came to compare the Word of God to the roaring thunder. The Lord will utter His voice thunderously from Jerusalem.

> "The message of Amos must have sounded like the roar of a lion capable of freezing its prey in its tracks (cf. Isa 5:25–30). As loud claps of thunder rattle buildings, so the word of the Lord through Amos startled and shook his audiences with its power. God's message delivered by his authorized messengers will always have an authentic ring and a startling effect."[x]

Along with the thunder comes the lightning. When the thunder of God's threatening is heard, the lightning of His judgment is imminent.[xi] And for that ancient, illiterate shepherd, it looked as if the sky were cracking so that a man could see the light of God beyond a solid dome. "The Lord utters His voice" and the impact will be terrific in this generation, according to Amos.

What a ridiculous time to speak of judgment. Why? Verse 1 informs us. Amos was speaking judgment in the days of King Uzziah. Speak judgment in the days of a Manasseh. Speak judgment in the does of an Ahab. But don't speak judgment in the days of Uzziah. Why? The very name "Uzziah" means "the Lord Jehovah is my strength."[xii] Of all of the kings of Judah, he was the most successful. The Philistines had been defeated on the west. The Arabs had been subjugated on the south. He fortified the walls of Jerusalem.[xiii] Why speak judgment in that happy context?

He mentions the king of the northern kingdom: Jeroboam (the son of Joash). The very name "Jeroboam" sounds like a political ticket: "let the people multiply."[xiv] The sanctuaries were filled from Dan to Bethel. If they didn't have a bus ministry, they must have had a camel ministry—the house was packed. The borders of Israel had been pressed to their uttermost extreme during the days of Jeroboam. The king's preacher will say, "Go home you sycamore fruit pitching (Amos 7:14), sheep-keeping Tekoan." We don't need you to remind us in the days of Jeroboam that there may be a quivering of the foundations and an underpinning of the very structure of society."

Any person who responded to God's judgment, accept for the narcotizing, anesthetizing, denial and numbness, are not here and not now. Whether it was the generation of Noah; or whether it was the generation of Belshazzar who was left in charge of the Babylonian Kingdom after his grandfather, Nebuchadnezzar, was gone; whether it was the Medo-Persians; none of them are here now because the clear, prophetic words from God explained that they would be destroyed.

Its not an easy thing to be an Amos. It is not a proper thing, and its not a polite thing. Amos was never elected to the ten most admired men of the Jerusalem Chamber of Commerce. I doubt it. It is not given to every man to speak in unsettled times, but it is given to some men to speak in times such as this.

What will this text look like? The habitations of the shepherds—the green pasturelands—will be shaken to the core via earthquake. These pasturelands, the very foundation of their economy, will be rocked. They will seer as if in a blast furnace.

I'm sure many who heard Amos speak of this impending judgment thought, "Well, surely there is an out. We can escape, can't we?" They may have thought about going to Carmel—the game preserve of Palestine.[xv] The affluent bureaucracy may have pondered scattering to their summer homes there. It was a place of wild animals and vegetation. They may have wanted to escape to Carmel, but Amos 1:2 teaches that the top of Carmel will wither.

The sap in the very trees will turn to ice at the sound of God's Word.

Neither in the pasturelands, nor on the peak of Carmel, will there be a place to avoid the fact that the lion has roared! God has thundered!

I'm really grateful Amos does not close the canon of Scriptures. We'd have very little for which to have good news. It would be difficult to give an invitation on the basis of Amos. What should I say, "Come meet the Lord, who is leaping on you, like a lion, in judgment." Sometimes, we make the mistake of thinking any one Word from God closes His message. Amos delivered a message from God just before God sent an earthquake.

I remember another earthquake. Do you? It is recorded in Matthew 28:2, *And behold, there was a great earthquake, for an angel of the Lord descended from heaven and came and rolled back the stone and sat on it.* Amos will speak later of darkness coming over his people. I remember an earthquake that shook in the darkness. It shook in the very city of David in which Amos lived. It occurred eight centuries later, when our Lord Jesus Christ became God's ultimate man during unsettled times in life. As the earth quaked, the tomb opened, and the sky darkened, Jesus died on the cross, and then He came back to life!

Dr. Jeremy Roberts

2 | TAKE A STAND FOR GOD

Amos 1:3–2

Amos' words remind us of a skilled weaver. Back and forth his words go around the neighboring nations of Israel in the eighth century (B.C.). East and west. North and south. Amos, the prophet of God, spins a web of prophecy and judgment as an indictment against the people that neighbor the people of God.

In the previous chapter, we began looking at the first of the writing prophets about Amos—the Tekoan—who heard that the Lord had roared from Zion. Amos had to declare what he heard the Lord say.

One of the burdens of the prophet that was Amos concerned the neighboring nations to the people of God. The thrust of the burden of the prophet spoke to their inhumanity, their barbarity, and to their (sometimes) atrocities. As national expressions. As political organizations. As governmental functions.

The God of Amos was not locked up in the sanctuary in Jerusalem. God turned loose on the world in the eighth century (B.C.). His concern was not exhausted with the order of service in the temple. He wasn't debating whether an organ or an electric guitar should be played. He is the God whose eyes run to and fro throughout the earth seeking out injustice that needed to be righted—barbarity that needed to be returned to humanity. And He was seeking out atrocities that needed the address of the judgment of a living God.

In days like our days that call out concern for justice, not only on a national level, but also on an international level, the message of Amos becomes contemporary. The thrust of Amos' message is that every national expression, every governmental organization, every political body stands before a living God who weighs that expression, that body, or that organization in the balance of his own judgment.

The presupposition of Amos' message to the international scene eight centuries before Christ is Amos' God belief that there is a common conscience among men in the presence or in the absence of God's self-disclosure thru biblical revelation. To contradict this common conscience of humanity is to involve oneself into what

Amos calls "transgression" which does not mean a revolt against a code of law nearly so much as it means "a personal offense to a living God."

6-17-18
J.R.

Amos looks at some obscure people: Syrians, Philistines, Phoenicians, Edomites, Ammonites, and other names that belong to footnotes in our generation, and he sees that the living God of Israel is consumed with passion. In the national and corporate life of people, he seeks that there would be humanity rather than barbarity. He seeks that there be justice rather than injustice. This was true for Amos, not only for the aged Rabbi as he sat studying the law, but also for the blood-curdling Ammonite in his paganism.

For Amos, God's response in the face of man's national and international inhumanity is swift and is sure. Far too often today, the judgment of God is viewed as His cataclysmic intervention at the end of history. When like lightning, God will intervene, and the heavens will crack, and God will bring history to a close. But the God of Amos was not an absentee God postponing His judgments until the end of history. The God of Amos was there in the midst of the presence of history in that generation, bringing about justice where it was needed and judgment where it was appropriate in the lives of men and in the lives of nations.

Amos uses the strange phrase over and over (v. 3), "For three transgressions of Damascus, and for four, I will not revoke the punishment." In that generation, the number *three* spoke of completeness, or fullness.[xvi] The fourth transgression was the climax insult to the living God.

Amos said that generation rested pivoting at the moment of the climax of God's intervention in the lives of the neighboring nations of Israel. In Hebrew, there is one word that stands for both *transgression* and for *God's response* in judgment: (*pěšaʿîm*).[xvii] To the Hebrew way of thinking, in the history of men and of nations, judgment and God's intervention follows so certainly the rebellion of man, that they are an inseparable unit even to the extent that one word can be used to express the complex of man's rebellion and God's intervention.

Isn't this a timely message? As we read the news about injustice and anarchy and terrorism, the evangelical Christian may sometimes want to cry out "Where is God?" in a world like ours. The first chapter of Amos gives the answer! He is not locked into a sanctuary. He is there in the midst of his world, judging, and seeing that justice and rectitude will be done within history.

Children that run away from home, or are abandoned by their parents, are nabbed by sex trafficking barbaric perverts and traded for prostitution and overall slavery. Where is God in this atrocity? He is judging and will see that justice and rectitude comes to pass.

Is God at all concerned with injustice? We see from the prophet Amos that the living God indeed is active in the affairs of men to see that that is so.

I. Stand Against Cruelty for the Good of Humanity

The God of Amos is active when there is an attitude of cruelty that reflects inhumanity of feeling. The City of Damascus was reputed by that generation to be the oldest in the world.[xviii] Amos turns his attention to the northern neighbors of Israel—the Syrians—whose empire and sphere of influence was symbolized by the capitol city, Damascus. Mohammed was so impressed with it that he said he would not enter the city of Damascus because a man should not enter paradise twice.[xix]

Amos had a different perspective of Damascus in the eighth century (B.C.). He leveled against it a withering indictment in Amos 1:3, *Thus says the* LORD: *"For three transgressions of Damascus, and for four, I will not revoke the punishment, because they have threshed Gilead with threshing sledges of iron . . ."*

Gilead was on the borderline between northern Israel and Syria. It was a buffer state, and in every battle, like Poland in modern Europe, it became the scene of battles of other people. It was like Alsace-Lorraine, between France and Germany, a tiny place that was doomed to suffer from the inhumanity and the cruelty of other people.[xx]

Where was the God of the earth when this was happening? Amos says He was there and was vigilant. Note how verse 3 speaks of those from Damascus threshing people with "sledges of iron." A particularly cruel and atrocious activity is cited in that day as grain was thrashed with boards seven feet long and three feet wide. Armed with jagged stones and piercing knives, these were weighted with stones and pulled by oxen like section harrows in a modern farm. But the Syrians had used these to rake over the writhing bodies of war refugees until they died in the sun of the Syrian Desert.[xxi] 2,800 years ago, where was God in all of this? Amos informed that generation that God was not absent, and neither would he be silent.

Amos informs that God will shortly speak. He will begin with a very political leadership that led out into the atrocity. Amos 1:4 says, *So I will send a fire upon the house of Hazael, and it shall devour the strongholds of Ben-hadad.*

These ancient names are significant in that the God of all the earth noted those who are responsible for inhumanity. The fire in this verse pertains to the fire of war and destruction.[xxii] It would consume the palace of the dynasty founded by Hazael, and now ruled by Ben-hadad III. That judgment that would begin with the leaders of this nation involved in barbarity would continue to its capital city and its defenses.

Amos 1:5a says, *I will break the gate-bar of Damascus.* The city of Damascus prided itself on the bronze bar of the gate that guarded the city.[xxiii] It was considered to be an impenetrable and impregnable defense.[xxiv] But the living God says that the city that maintains itself by barbarity and inhumanity will be defenseless in the onslaught of the judgment of God worked out in history.

Having passed from the leaders to the capital city, Amos culminates these words by looking at the population itself. Continuing in verse 5, ". . . and cut off the inhabitants from the Valley of Aven . . ." "The

Valley of Aven" means a plain of wealth or a wealthy suburb of the city of Damascus.[xxv] Continuing in verse 5, ". . . and him who holds the scepter from Beth-eden . . ." The very name "Eden" itself means "the house of pleasure."[xxvi] Well, the people there will not experience much more pleasure as they, too will be cut off. Those who sat at the breakfast table and read the Damascus Observer while learning about the incident at Gilead and said, "Isn't that too bad? What are we going to do to amuse ourselves today?" They, too, will hear a word from the Lord.

Amos informs us that when nations, in their expressions, when governments in their organizations, when people in their corporate activities become barbaric, God intervenes.

The last part of verse 5 is most striking to me. We are told that, according to the Lord, "the people of Syria shall go into exile to Kir." The city of Kir was in Mesopotamia.[xxvii] What this amounts to is a reversal of their history. The Syrians had come out of that great area between the two rivers, and now because they have become a people of barbarity, God would send them back.

Was Amos a mad man? Was he a pessimist? Did his words fall fruitless? Not in the least. These words spoken in 751 B.C. came to be fulfilled in 732 B.C. when that unusually named Assyrian ruler, Tiglath Pileser, leveled the city of Damascas and carried its inhabitants back from whence they came, and canceled their history.[xxviii]

What is the application of these ancient words in your life? Such acts of barbarity may seem far-fetched to Americans. The word is that God holds accountable entire nations—Christian or pagan—when they become a people that commit atrocities. We may even feel a comfortable distance from this condemnation, but the eternal principle here reveals that God's settled disposition in history is that He is against inhumanity and barbarity. He will see that in the processes of history, those who live in barbarity may well also perish.

If we cannot externalize these words, we can internalize them. Our words and our acts can have jagged edges just like those stony, sharp instruments of the ancient Syrians. There is a word to us about our own disposition. There is also a Lord who Amos never knew who taught us in his manifesto, the Sermon on the Mount, that inhumanity and barbarity, not only of action, but of thought, is forbidden by those who live in His kingdom.

Where is the God of Amos? He is right there in the midst of the international scene, and He is working out justice on His own timetable.

II. Stand for Life in the Face of Adversity

Amos turns from the neighboring nation to the north to the neighboring nation to the southwest in his next word to the nations. He speaks a word about contempt for human personality. The ancient Philistines were the southwestern neighbors of Amos' generation. He addresses their principle city—Gaza. It's a city that has given its name to her contemporary geographical location. Gaza represents the five affluent and wealthy cities of the ancient Philistines. Amos has a word of indictment for them and it concerns contempt for human personality.

Amos 1:6 says, *Thus says the* LORD: *'For three transgressions of Gaza, and for four, I will not revoke the punishment, because they carried into exile a whole people to deliver them up to Edom.'* Once again, strange, ancient, obscure places, but the significance is this: The Philistines were on the slave trade route between Egypt to the south and Syria to the north. It had become a way of life for them to trade the tiny, neighboring Judean villages, and to carry away as Amos emphasizes the "whole of the population." There would be an eerie cry in the darkness of the night in the scream of innocent children and frantic mothers as villages were carried away to be sold in the slave trade.

Where is the God of Israel? Is he only concerned with the incense that is burned in the temple and the sacrifices that roast on the altar? Not in the least. He is right there overseeing and involved in the history of those who exploit others and are inhumane and barbaric and who hold human personality in contempt.

Amos says that punishment will surely come for those whose nation is built on contempt for human personality.

Amos 1:7 says, *⁷ So I will send a fire upon the wall of Gaza, and it shall devour her strongholds.* In 734 B.C., it did.ˣˣⁱˣ Then, verse 8a says, *⁸ I will cut off the inhabitants from Ashdod.* It is amazing. In 711 B.C., it came to pass. Amos 8:b says, *and him who holds the scepter from Ashkelon; I will turn my hand against Ekron,* In 701 B.C., that came to pass. The last section of verse 8 says, *'and the remnant of the Philistines shall perish,' says the Lord GOD.* Have you met a Philistine lately? Of course you haven't. They have perished!

The Lord has a settled disposition to judge in history those who live by contempt for the humanity of others.

NATIONALLY

Very practically, what is the application of this? Well, nationally, there is an application: Any nation that bills itself for contempt for human personality will perish under the judgment of God.

It was David Livingston who cried out against the slave raids of Zanzabar when peaceful tribes were baited and carried throughout jungles waiting for ships. If we were to hear these words from Amos for us, we might need to paraphrase it. Just like the man who wrote the book at the peak of modern racial battles in America, *Prophets on Main Street*,[xxx] in cities such as Atlanta, Jackson, and Little Rock, "I will not turn back the punishment thereof, for they have built their greatness with innumerable indignities and contempt for others."

We can only hope that in our own national process that the grace of God has intervened in time that we will not face the inevitable rendezvous with God if we build our society on contempt for any other human beings.

INDIVIDUALLY

There is also a word for us individually from this passage: For the disposition of God is against any individual who lives out his life in contempt for any other human beings. It was said of Jesus' generation that they actually walked *around* Samaria. However, Jesus knew He had to walk *through* Samaria (Jn 4:1–45). Jesus gave us an example that we are not to live out our days in contempt for the humanity of other people, whoever our own Samaritans may happen to be.

III. Stand for What is Right in the Temptation of Neutrality

Amos turns, finally, to look to the west. We'll go with him there. He looks at another ancient, neighboring nation: The Phoenicians. You may remember them—sailors and ship builders. He addresses them in Amos 1:9 by speaking to their capitol city, Tyre. He knew what we have come to learn. Amos learned the same thing that we have come to learn: The spirit of the capitol city will saturate the nation. So, speaking to the part for the whole, he speaks to Tyre.

Amos 1:10–11 says, *¹⁰ So I will send a fire upon the wall of Tyre, and it shall devour her strongholds.*" *¹¹ Thus says the* LORD: *"For three transgressions of Edom, and for four, I will not revoke the punishment, because he pursued his*

brother with the sword and cast off all pity, and his anger tore perpetually, and he
kept his wrath forever.

When Amos looks to the west, he pronounces God's judgment on the people who played the middleman at the expense of others. The Phoenicians had not thrashed or harrowed refugees to death. Nor had they raided villages and carried away slaves. They simply let their place serve as the neutral staging ground for many of these things to take place. They were not experiencing the sin of commission, but the sin of omission. They omitted standing up for what was right in the midst of wrongness. They played the middleman at the expense of others.

The God who actively speaks out against those who are inhumane, or barbaric, or who perpetrate atrocities and injustices, has a word to those who say, "Well, we were just caught in the middle of the situation." God's words concerning His judgment are, "I will not revoke the punishment."

It took a century for Amos' word about Tyre to come to pass. It was not until 664 B.C. that the Assyrians, under Ashurbanipal, overwhelmed that city.[xxxi] It messed up by straddling the fence at the expense of others.

There is a word here for us. Has not our generation seen leaders across our land claim time and time again, "I was caught in the middle, and I was not responsible." Perhaps the lengthy-cast shadow of a Pontius Pilate, caught between a Christ whom he feared, and Jews whom he feared more, said "I wish my hands of this matter" (Matt 27:24–26).

The prophecy of Amos is a call to national and individual responsibility. The God of Amos is not a God who will accept our feeble, "Excuse me. I was caught in the middle." He is the God with the plumb line in His hand measuring His people to see that they always act out of responsibility.

There is another message to this ancient city of Tyre. This is the first word to all of these nations that doesn't involve the people of God. In the message to Damascas, the Syrians were attacking northern Israel. In the message to the Philistines, they were attacking Judah. Here, the living God is concerned with inhumanity one pagan to another. The Phoenicians were blood-curdling, Baal-worshiping pagans. Yet, the living God, even there, is active for humanity.

We must not disenfranchise most of the civilized world. We must understand that the God we meet to worship is the God of international history. Everywhere in His creation, there is cruelty and insensitivity of contempt for inhumanity. There are middlemen who exist at the expense of others. God is not silent and is not still.

CONCLUSION

It is our confession that in the processes of history and as He consummates in our Lord Jesus Christ, He will see that justice is done among men and among nations. But as we discussed last Sunday morning, Amos does not close the canon of Scriptures. Sometimes, it would be difficult to give an invitation on that basis.

Amos has spoken to us about atrocities and cruelties in ancient history. Our Lord who was very much in view with the spirit of Amos said that neutrality and paralysis is not enough. *If a man would ask for your cloak, give him your coat also* (Matt 5:40). *If a man would compel you to go one mile, go an extra* (Matt 5:41–42) . . . *If a man strikes you on the cheek, turn the other* (Matt 5:39).

We have a mandate far more compelling than Amos could ever imagine. He hoped for a world where people wouldn't kill each other left and right. Our Lord is the Lord over a kingdom where we're commanded to have a delicacy of feeling, a sensitivity of justice, and even Amos could not imagine it.

Who is equal to these things? Only those who know Jesus Christ as Lord of history and who come to know Him in the forgiveness that gives us a base from which to go out and live, setting right what has been wrong, making humane where there has been cruelty, and being gentle where there has been brutality. If we know a Lord like that, we can live like an Amos in our generation.

3 | CHOSEN FOR RESPONSIBILITY

Amos 3

I recently attended a meeting of primarily African-American pastors and was reminded of the wonderful cadence and response that existed among the pastors who were present. In antiphony, in rapport, the preacher and congregation continually responded to one another. We can learn a great deal therefrom.

With the temple slow and the speaking low, punctuated by an occasional amen. Prodded on by this encouragement, the crescendo begins to grow, and there are responses: "Preach on!" and "That's Right!" And then finally, in a feverish tempo, between people and preacher, it seems the very house would totter upon its foundations. This kind of antiphonal response, back and forth, between preacher and people, has a hallowed tradition. For it was the case in the days of Amos—the prophet of Tekoa. He was masterful in his use of audience response. Back and forth between Amos and those who listened to him, there came the Word of the Lord and their response.

We heard this firstly in chapter one as Amos indicted the enemies of God's covenant people. One by one, Edom will fall under the judgment of God and his audience said, "Amen." He looked to the north as he mentioned Damascus and Syria and people said, "Preach on!" But what a devastating consequence when Amos moves from the circumference to the center as he levees judgment with the very people listening to him.

Once again, in the third chapter of his prophecy, Amos uses the response between preacher and people. He begins low and slow. He speaks to them of common matters about which they would agree with him.

Amos' audience sat in smug self-congratulation that they were the people of God with immunity from God's judgment. After all, we have Abraham as our father and the covenant of Sinai as our heritage. Amos begins with them in a devastating way that leads to a crescendo and a climax that catches them absolutely off guard.

I. Amos Speaks of the Law of Cause and Result in the Spiritual World

Amos was a rural man speaking to the land in peasantry in the northern kingdom. He knew how to play upon them with words which would illicit from them positive response. He does this in verses 3–8 of this third chapter.

World of Men

He first deduces from the world of men: *³ Do two walk together, unless they have agreed to meet?* This is in reference to two men meeting one another in the desolate, deserted desert around Tekoa. That was an absolute impossibility and a total unlikelihood unless they had agreed to meet there. Men met in that desert no more often than ships pass in open sea. There you have it. Cause and result from a familiar sphere of experience. The result: they meet in the desert. The assumed cause: they agreed to do so. Then, Amos' listeners said, "Yes. That's the way it is."

Then, from the experiences of men, particularly shepherds, he deduces two things in verse 4. Look at verse 4a: *Does a lion roar in the forest, when he has no prey?* Do you hear the piercing roar of the ravenous lion splitting through the night when you're a shepherd and you already know that he has leaped on a defenseless and helpless sheep? Cause and result. You hear the result. The roar of the lion in mid-flight caused jaws to drop. The people to whom Amos was communicating had to have been saying, "Amen. Preach on preacher!"

Then, in the latter half of verse 4, he cried out, Does a young lion cry out from his den, if he has taken nothing? Many times, they heard the low and satisfied growl of the cub who had filled himself. That was the result. The cause was that he had eaten his safety. Once again, they say, "Yes, Amos. We know about these causes and these results."

World of the Hunter

Next, he moves to the world of the hunter. This was a familiar world to his listeners. Look at verse 5: *Does a bird fall in a snare on the earth, when there is no trap for it? Does a snare spring up from the ground, when it has taken nothing?* You know that someone has unleashed a snare and pulled it down. It caused a result. A bird plummets to the earth because someone has snatched him.

And again the people say to Amos, "Oh yes. We have seen that many times." The result is that something springs up from the ground because something has been caught. Once again, as the momentum builds, Amos' listeners say, "Yes. We know about cause and result in our experience as hunters."

Then, in verse 6, Amos moves to something more subtle: Is a trumpet blown in a city, and the people are not afraid? When the elder in the village sounds the shofar and the ram's horn, there is general alarm in the city.[xxxii] His congregation begins to shift uneasily because they now realize he is speaking to them. Verse 6 reverses the emphasis: The cause is given (blowing of the ram's horn). So, there is alarm in the city.

Now, Amos is honing in on his target in verse 8: *The lion has roared; who will not fear? The Lord GOD has spoken; who can but prophesy?* You who admit that there is cause and result in the world of man and in the world of nature must come to see that there is cause and result in the spiritual world.

The Lord has roared from Zion! It is inevitable that Amos will proclaim the Lord's message. He cannot help but do so.

Then, Amos moves to his point. The second verse of this chapter likely followed these other verses as it was preached. *You only have I known of all the families of the earth…* This is the essence of Amos' message. It is the distillation of everything he says: Yahweh, Jehovah, the covenant God speaks. "You only have I known of all the families of the earth." What could a statement like that mean?

Word Study of *KNOW*

Certainly the word "know" here does not have its cognitive value that God was only aware of Israel and not the other nations. That word, *yāda'tî,* rather, bears its full relational meaning, "You, Israel, alone, have I *intimately* known . . . have I *watched over* . . . have I *committed myself to* . . . of all the families of the earth."[xxxiii] It is that same Hebrew word that is used to describe an experiential knowledge of a man and woman together. "You alone, Israel, have I elected, have I intimately given myself to." That is the cause.

Now, Amos' hearers knew the result. They had been schooled

through generations of training. The result: You only have I known of all the families of the earth. Therefore, you have immunity from judgment. You have a guarantee of rescue. You have a promise of perpetuity.

Then, like a bolt out of the blue, Amos shatters them with the result that follows from that cause. "You alone have I known of all the families of the earth; therefore, I will punish you for all your iniquities." They were thunderstruck. Their mouths dropped. For they had agreed with every cause and result that Amos had spoken as he set up the momentum. Now, they're ready to agree with Amos, but then he devastates them. When God intimately watches over and gives himself to one people, he will punish all of their iniquities when they become an irresponsible people. That was heresy for Amos' generation, but oh what a compelling spiritual truth is found in those words. It has gripped my heart. It has given me a new vista on the church today.

God is the limiting God who chooses to redeem the whole by limiting Himself to a small part.

- He chose Abraham as the one man out of Ur (Gen 12:1–20).

- He chose the slave nation (Israel) as the one nation out of other nations (Deut 7:6–7).

Amos reminds them that just because God redeems the whole by limiting Himself to the part, just for that very reason, when His people become irresponsible, He must speak to them in judgment as well as speaking to them in grace. God will not be without a demonstration of His righteousness through His covenant people.

If they respond positively, He will respond in His grace to them. But if they respond to Him negatively and irresponsibly, He will demonstrate His righteousness through judgment. God will not be left without a people through whom to demonstrate His righteousness and His holiness if they are a responsible people, a demonstration of grace. If they are an irresponsible people like Amos' generation, nevertheless they will be God's people and they will demonstrate His righteousness as a history of judgment. To whom much is given, much is required.

The art critic will not judge the finger-painting of an elementary child with the same measure that he will critique the painting of the master artist. To whom, much has been given, and from him much will be required. He will know the sterner possibility and the sterner judgment.

The little boy hammering together his first two by fours will not be judged because they do not meet at a right angle because little has been given to him. However, the master carpenter has the greater possibility and the greater judgment when laid alongside his hammerings together. There is the right angle that tests whether this is indeed square.

So it is with God's covenant people. What a devastating result from the cause. "You alone have I known of all the families of the earth; therefore, I will punish you for all your iniquities." For Amos to be chosen by God is to enter into the awesome possibility of grace, but it is entered into the total devastation of judgment when God's covenant people become irresponsible. May I observe this, too. Amos pointed to his generation, that cause and result is effective in the spiritual world just as it is effective in every other arena of man's experience.

- A chemist will tell you that given sodium and chloride in the right combination and under the right circumstances, salt will be farmed invariably.
- A biologist will tell you that when chromosomes in a cell align themselves within certain configuration, that it is a law of biology that division will take place.

- An astronomer will tell you that when there is a certain conjunction of the heavenly bodies, given effects will take place.
- A physicist will tell you that for every action, there is an equal and opposite reaction.

We live in a world that is governed by cause and effect. Except we fool ourselves that there is not cause and effect in the spiritual world.

Amos reminded his generation of simple, rural, peasant people that just as they observed cause and result in their world, so was there cause and result in life lived responsibly or irresponsibly under God. Oh, how it has gripped me that in God's church today, in the covenant community of the New Testament, God will be vindicated in His righteousness. He will be vindicated as He blesses us in grace because He has known us alone as His covenant people. Or, He will be vindicated as He knows us in judgment. He will demonstrate Himself through His chosen people.

II. When God's Chosen People Become Irresponsible, Even their Pagan Enemies Can Indict Them

Amos was a clever preacher. No one would have slept on him.

Amos' secret to homiletical excellence is that he pricked the ears of his listeners after devastating them with this argument of cause and result. He told them to prepare for a state visit.

Remember, he is speaking to the capitol city of the northern kingdom, Samaria, the home of the bureaucracy, the pride, the capitol, the seat of power. He told them to prepare for a state visit in verse 9a: *Proclaim to the strongholds in Ashdod and to the strongholds in the land of Egypt, and say, "Assemble yourselves on the mountains of Samaria . . ."* This would have caught the attention of Amos' self-congratulatory listeners. A state visit! Their very enemies were coming to visit. They had to have been excited in their anticipation.

The city of Samaria is in an amphitheater.[xxxiv] They were surrounded by mountains on which people could look down and into the city. The enemies of Israel—the Phoenicians, the Egyptians—were invited to come and stand around the circumference of this amphitheater and to look down on the capital city of Samaria.[xxxv]

Do you remember the old western movies? This was just like the Indians that were hiding behind the sand dunes and looking down at the cowboys beneath. Oh, what a consequence comes from this anticipated state visit. In the mouths of the pagan neighbors come these indictments as they look down upon Samaria and the covenant people of God.

Verse 9b says, *and see the great tumults within her, and the oppressed in her midst.* When the Egyptians and the Phoenicians—not exactly bywords for civility—looked down upon the city of Samaria, they say, "What confusion of might over right." They say, "What oppression! How justice has been turned to injustice. How morality has been turned to immorality." They mouthed the very indictments that Amos gives throughout his prophecy.

Women had become a disgrace for their society in the fourth chapter. Courts had become so corrupt that justice could not be found in the fifth chapter. A capitol city had become so proud of itself that it almost stumbled the sixth chapter. And trade and commerce had become so dishonest, no one could be sure that he was buying what he paid for in the eighth chapter.

Oh, what a word from Amos. When God's covenant people become irresponsible, even their enemies look down and blush at what they see.

The most devastating word is saved for the mouth of the Lord Himself in verse 10: *"They do not know how to do right," declares the* LORD. This literally means that they have forgotten how to do what is right.[xxxvi] The Hebrew word translated as *right* means "straightforward, upright, a straight line," meaning they have become incapacitated from doing that which is straightforward.[xxxvii] A generation of injustice and oppression led to people who mouthed in the face of their heritage, "We do not want to know the will of a covenant God." Their judgment is that they got their wish. They forgot how to do right. They became incapable of the distinction between justice and injustice. They had no clue what was moral or immoral. Could it still be the case that the enemies of God's people could gather around and indict those?

Is it possible that the enemies of God's covenant people could yet, even still, look down upon them and bring an indictment?

The communist Chinese have gone on record with their puritanical society.[xxxviii] They're straight-laced and straight-forward as they indict us (Americans) for our movies and television programs, and our magazines with their constant suggestive, voyeuristic, and inappropriate interests.

Let us hear from Amos! When God's covenant people lose their responsibility, even their enemies may stand up to indict them.

III. When God's People Become Irresponsible, the Only Response is Judgment

Amos' listeners did not like this message any more than a contemporary man would like it. They said, "Amos, you sheep-keeping, rural peasant, go back. We've got our view on these things. God has guaranteed us immunity because we are His people. God has promised us rescue." So, Amos pictures them as they dally around on their overstuffed high horses in verse 12:

Thus says the LORD: "As the shepherd rescues from the mouth of the lion two legs, or a piece of an ear, so shall the people of Israel who dwell in Samaria be rescued, with the corner of a couch and part of a bed. That's an interesting verse. It simply means they were lollygagging around on overstuffed ottomans and are covered with the lace of Damascus while chanting, "The Lord is our shepherd, we shall not want." And Amos said, "Oh yes. For your generation, the Lord is a shepherd indeed, but this is the kind of shepherd He is: As the shepherd rescues from the mouth of the lion two legs, or a piece of an ear."

What a devastating word! This is really a Proverb illustrating one thing by another. I understand that in that day, when a shepherd would lose an animal to a beast, he had to produce whatever was left to show the owner of the sheep that he had not really stolen it or sold it.[xxxix] Amos, in a rather rustic way, was never bothered by the crudity he used to explain his point. As the shepherd rescues from the mouth of the lion two legs, or a piece of an ear.

Amos closes this word with a message about the day of the Lord in verse 14. In his apocalyptic vision, he moves forward to the time when the judgment of which he speaks is consummated. Amos uses the phrase at the beginning of verse 14 "on the day," but he doesn't define it. It was ominous and looming over people who must brace themselves for it's coming if there is not repentance.

Look at verse 15: *I will strike the winter house along with the summer house, and the houses of ivory shall perish, and the great houses shall come to an end," declares the LORD.*

The key word becomes "house"—"judgment." On the house of Jacob—Bethel—the house of God—the winter house, summer house, ivory house, great house. Amos sees in the monuments they have built with beam upon beam the oppression of an unjust society, and he says that judgment will begin there. There, at Bethel, the house of God. And the winter house and the summer house whereby extortion, a few will live in luxury while others live in a distorted and perverted society of injustice and malignancy toward the "have nots." The ivory house, houses in-laid with ivory, such have been discovered. The great house shall have an end, says the Lord.

What do we say about this word from Amos? Verse 15 ends with no gospel . . . no good news. Amos has a bit of good news in his last chapter when he speaks of the future that God promises. In various ways and many parts to our fathers by the prophets, but in this last day, he has spoken in his son.

And this side of Christ, we know things about judgment that Amos never knew. We know the seriousness with which God takes judgment because we see the cross of Christ turned into the judgment seat of God. The cross is nothing other than God taking the judgment of the end of history and moving it back into the center of history so we can see both the seriousness of His judgment and His grace.

Yes, the cross of Christ shows us the seriousness of judgment about which Amos spoke. So does the coming of the Holy Spirit. John the Baptist said, in Matthew 3:11, *I baptize you with water for repentance, but he who is coming after me is mightier than I, whose sandals I am not worthy to carry. He will baptize you with the Holy Spirit and fire.*

Now, we like the Spirit, but we question the fire. The Holy Spirit comes in judgment to the covenant people of God. Burning out our dross. Consuming our impurity. Leaving us sterling in His sight.

We cannot do what Amos did any more. Amos, in the circle of the prophets, seemed to hear voices we no longer hear. They knew about Armies marching, earthquakes shaking, and cities calling, and they predicted it with accuracy. We can no longer do that, and I would add poignantly, it would be a prostitution of the pulpit when we try to do so today.

That was the prophetic gift.[xl] That specificity. We have to speak a more general word about man, sin, and judgment, but we have a word that Amos never had. We have the cross of Christ, where God took the brunt of judgment upon Himself so that in the Christ event, we see that the hand that holds the gavel is also the nail-scarred hand. Amos didn't see that.

We must be wounded before we can be healed. There must be an Amos as well as the wounded healer of Isaiah's suffering servant. God smites us with the left hand of an Amos. He lifts us up again at Calvary by smiting Himself. God was in Christ, reconciling the world to Himself.

4 | CLINGING TO GOD DURING DISTURBING TIMES

Amos 4

Often, we have had the common experience of standing outside a door upon which the sign "do not disturb" was posted outside. I've noticed that these signs are now posted in several languages so that no one misunderstands that the parties involved do not want to be disturbed. The truth is that many of us want to hang "Do Not Disturb" signs outside of many dimensions of our lives.

Some have hung "Do Not Disturb" signs outside their past. Others have hung "Do Not Disturb" signs when thinking about the future. We love to paint that sign over the personal aspects of our lives—Do Not Disturb!

Many would like to hang that on the doorknob of the church—Do Not Disturb Us! That's not always bad because the church sometimes needs to focus on their needs, but if this happens often, it becomes *disturbing*.

However, the prophet Amos had a way of communicating in his fourth chapter that sometimes our church needs to be both *disturbed* and *disturbing*. Amos had the sticky habit of unlocking the living God from the sanctuary of Israel. And unleashing him into the commonplaces of society, Amos turned loose God out of the sanctuary on the affluent, urban commercial men of the capitol city of the northern kingdom—Samaria. And he also turned loose God on their wives in this fourth chapter of his prophecy.

The popular preachers of Amos' days were like the popular preachers of every generation. They basically told people the good news. They especially enjoyed telling people what they wanted to hear. I don't know if they would constantly stand up and tell people, "Something good is going to happen to you." They certainly gave a message that was always positive. It took a lot of poor and positive, rustic and bucolic men like Amos to tell that generation the truth.

Something very bad was about to happen. They did not begin to live responsibly before God. I wish I could make the message of Amos more palatable. I wish I could sugar coat it so the faithful flock would indeed see it was easier to take. But the message of Amos does defy that. Amos does tell us when the church should be disturbed and when it should become disturbing.

I. Cling to God When Women Lose their Sense of Worth (vv. 1–5)

In the first three verses of this fourth chapter of Amos, the prophet turns from his withering indictment of men of commerce and men of justice to focus his attention on the women. Pointedly, the women who live in the affluence of the urban center of the capitol city of the northern kingdom—Samaria.

His word to them was descriptive and interpretive. Hear this word of peril, crying out in the marketplace, where the women of the city would be shopping in the stalls and the booths that sold produce and meat. "Hear this word!" Amos perils. And they turn to hear this rustic, bucolic fellow from down south as he addresses their eager faces with this word.

Amos 4:1–3 says, *Hear this word, you cows of Bashan, who are on the mountain of Samaria, who oppress the poor, who crush the needy, who say to your husbands, 'Bring, that we may drink!'* [2] *The Lord GOD has sworn by his holiness that, behold, the days are coming upon you, when they shall take you away with hooks, even the last of you with fishhooks.* [3] *And you shall go out through the breaches, each one straight ahead; and you shall be cast out into Harmon," declares the LORD.*

Look at the first verse. It calls the women of Bashan "cows." Bashan was a trans-Jordanian area that was well known for its fertility. Its soil was that of disintegrating lava that produces sleek and beautiful cattle. It is to these that Amos likens the urban, affluent women of his generation.

Now, you must understand that Amos' words to his generation were not as crude as they sound to us. Sometimes, this sort of speech in the Old Testament was used flatteringly of the women. In the Song of Solomon, that is the case. In Song of Solomon 5:5b, the wise man describes a woman by saying, *Your hair is like a flock of goats leaping down the slopes of Gilead.* I can just imagine going up to my wife and saying "Hey baby. Nice goat hair. Hot! Bahhh!"

When Amos uses this phrase, he does not mean it as that of flattery. He means that the women had become animalistic, insensitive, and brutish. And remember that he is not talking to pagans. He is talking to women who were reared in the good and genteel homes of the religious capitol. These were the women who had the heritage of the best of the Old Testament. And yet within one generation of urban affluence, they had been obsessed with luxury. They had become insensitive toward anything in life other than the brutish and the animalistic.

He characterizes these women with a three-fold indictment at the end of verse 1: who oppress the poor, who crush the needy, who say to your husbands, 'Bring, that we may drink!'

Amos, speaking to the women of that generation, sees in them and in their petulant disrespect of their husbands, part of the problem in the society of Israel is that they oppress the poor. In their elaborate and unfounded and groundless and voracious appetite for more of an affluent life, they have led their husbands to become fraudulent in dealing with those who work for them.

Some of your versions of the Bible use the word "masters" instead of "husbands" in Amos 4:1. This is because the women were telling their husbands what to do. This is an unbiblical structure of a marriage. Church, neither you nor I should *tell* anyone what to do. We should *ask* them to do something. In this scenario, it would be analogous to a wife calling a husband while in his office suite atop a building in downtown Greenville and saying, "Hurry! Bring home a six-pack. I haven't had a drink all day long."

Keep in mind the first three chapters were withering, scorching indictments pointed toward the men. So, what is God's attitude toward all of this? Amos says it is one of vehement judgment. Look at Amos 4:2a, *The Lord GOD has sworn by his holiness that, behold, the days are coming upon you . . .* That's the greatest oath the Lord God can take. The epitome of His personality—holiness—was put on the line so that the brutish and insensitive lifestyle will be judged.

The time of judgment is left ominous and foreboding. The day shall come, but he does not know when. They loom there on the horizon. "The days are coming upon you . . ." when an insensitive society will face the living God.

Amos paints the picture of the women of Samaria falling under the judgment of an invading army. Incidentally, the picture that Amos paints is exactly that which archaeologists have discovered with the unearthed the remnants of the Assyrian society.[xli] The Assyrians were the conquerors of those to whom Amos prophesied within decades of his prophecy. Amos pictures the women of the capitol being led out of the breached and ruined walls of a defeated city with rings in their noses and through their lips like fish jerked out of the hospitable environment of water and into the cold brightness of day.

These who have become insensitive and brutish while enjoying their luxuries and affluence will suddenly find themselves jerked out of their habitual environment. Those who had been proud and disdainful, like the sleek cattle of Bashan, suddenly find themselves like fish on the end of a hook. Amos certainly had a way with words, and that is how it came to pass.

The Hebrew prophets, Amos, and particularly Isaiah, had the insight born of observation and of the spirit of God that it is the women of any society that become the barometer for the moral and spiritual temperature of that society.

In Pastor R.G. Lee's description of Jezebel in his famous sermon, "Payday Someday" he said these words: "When women love vulgarity more than virtue, when they love mirrors more than manners, when they love adornment more than adoration of the living God, it makes an impact."[xlii]

A woman may become a Lucrezia Borgia, who at the lowest point of the medieval papacy dragged down the papacy to its lowest point.[xliii] On the other hand, a woman may become a Florence Nightingale who pours out her life in the Crimea, and then retires to London, and according to Cecil Woodham-Smith, the biographer, she so enchanted Queen Victoria that again and again called for Florence Nightingale to be her chamber guest.[xliv] So fascinated was she with the noble character of that woman. A woman has the opportunity to become a Cleopatra that pulls down an empire, or an Elizabeth Browning who enables the life of a middle-aged man and of a whole era of society.[xlv]

You may say, "Oh pastor. You're just passing the buck onto the women." No! You say, "Preacher, you're just like Adam, in the garden, who said 'Well, the woman you gave me, she made me eat it.'" No! I'm saying this, and Amos acknowledges it, that when the women of a society become insensitive and brutish, it means the men have long been gone and the last vestige of sensitivity has been crushed.

It is the temperament of a woman sensitive with injustice, to be sympathetic with oppression, to be open to that which is hurt, but these women gave themselves to other things. Amos was giving a word of warning to women who have lost their sense of worth.

You can almost hear the people crying out, "What about our church services?" Things may not be where they ought to there, but look at our worship . . . it is so beautiful. Amos has a word about worthless worship.

We've come to see that Amos was a rather surprising sort of preacher. In the previous chapter we saw that Amos was able to get the crowd going with some "Amen's" and solid response before knocking them back on their heels. However, none of his devices were more striking than the one in verse 4. He mimicked the preachers in their holiest sanctuaries: Bethel and Gilgal. He mimicks their ministerial wine when he says, "Come to Bethel."

They were used to hearing the words "Come to Bethel, and the Lord will thoroughly bless your life." Amos 4:4a says, *Come to Bethel, and transgress; to Gilgal, and multiply transgression.* It was the next thing to blasphemy. It was irreverence and a parody of their nation. They would point to their worship and say "Yes. The very worship of this kind of society has become rebellion."

Religious activism was at an all-time high. He points this out in Amos 4:4b, *bring your sacrifices every morning,* They were supposed to bring their sacrifices once per year, but in their activism, they brought them daily.

The end of Amos 4:4 says, *your tithes every three days;* Every three years, they were supposed to bring their tithes, but these people had become scrupulous. Every third day, they would bring their tithes to the sanctuary.

Amos 5:5a says, *offer a sacrifice of thanksgiving of that which is leavened,* The emphasis is on the expense of this offering. Not only to offer their sacrifice, but also to give costly yeast. But Amos touches their motive when he says, in Amos 5:5b, *and proclaim freewill offerings, publish them; for so you love to do, O people of Israel!' declares the Lord GOD.* God was telling these people that they were being ostentatious as they gave their tithes.

Remember the words of Jesus in Matthew 6:5, *But when you pray, go into your room and shut the door and pray to your Father who is in secret. And your Father who sees in secret will reward you.*

These people had become obsessed with the aesthetic duty of the worship services. They were intoxicated with the great crowds that came to the sanctuary. This very obsession is one of the best insulations against confrontation with the living God. When the elements of worship, the aesthetics of worship, the routine of worship comes to the center, and the experience of meeting with God is pressed to the periphery, we are insulated from an encounter with God.

What are some of the marks of the religion Amos indicted?

- Quantity over quality
- Form and ceremony over content
- Ritual over experience with God
- Worship becomes an end itself instead of a meeting with a transcendent God

They had displaced God as the center of worship, and God was about to displace them. Activism, religiously, was at an all-time high. But in God's view, the vital faith of the people was at an all-time low. Cluttered calendars religiously do not necessarily equate to spiritual vitality.

The best way that a congregation can be sure this is never the verdict of God on us is to hear the word of Amos and let it be a warning—a signpost to make us divinely uneasy and perpetually uncomfortable lest ritual replace experience, lest form replace content in our worship and our work.

II. Cling to God When His Warnings Are Ignored (vv. 6 – 10)

> [6] *"I gave you cleanness of teeth in all your cities, and lack of bread in all your places, yet you did not return to me," declares the* LORD. [7] *"I also withheld the rain from you when there were yet three months to the harvest; I would send rain on one city, and send no rain on another city; one field would have rain, and the field on which it did not rain would wither;* [8] *so two or three cities would wander to another city to drink water, and would not be satisfied; yet you did not return to me," declares the* LORD. [9] *"I struck you with blight and mildew; your many gardens and your vineyards, your fig trees and your olive trees the locust devoured; yet you did not return to me," declares the* LORD. [10] *"I sent among you a pestilence after the manner of Egypt; I killed your young men with the sword, and carried away your horses, and I made the stench of your camp go up into your nostrils; yet you did not return to me," declares the* LORD. [11] *"I overthrew some of you, as when God overthrew Sodom and Gomorrah, and you were as a brand plucked out of the burning; yet you did not return to me," declares the* LORD. [12] *"Therefore thus I will do to you, O Israel; because I will do this to you, prepare to meet your God, O Israel!"*

Amos runs through a list, a litany, of God's judgments upon Israel. Five different times, after issuing a warning, God says, "Yet you did not return to me."

What were God's warnings?

A. Famine (v. 6)

6 "I gave you cleanness of teeth in all your cities, and lack of bread in all your places, yet you did not return to me," declares the LORD.

They considered nature to be their domain that would allow recreation, food, and clothing. However, God had the propensity to turn this thing against them.

B. Drought (vv. 7–8)

7 "I also withheld the rain from you when there were yet three months to the harvest; I would send rain on one city, and send no rain on another city; one field would have rain, and the field on which it did not rain would wither;

God was explaining that He was going to withhold those bursts of winter rain that usually matured their crops. God did it in a unique way. He did it so that it was evident He was at work. He would allow rain to fall on one plot of land, but not another. Like gerrymandering lines, it would happen in one place, but not another.

It seems evident that in some places God would withhold rain upon the just and the unjust alike, but still there was no response.

C. Ruined Food (v. 9)

[9] *"I struck you with blight and mildew; your many gardens and your vineyards, your fig trees and your olive trees the locust devoured; yet you did not return to me," declares the LORD.*

D. Epidemic and War (v. 10)

This Egyptian pestilence came from the Nile Delta. It was something like Malaria.

[10] *"I sent among you a pestilence after the manner of Egypt; I killed your young men with the sword, and carried away your horses, and I made the stench of your camp go up into your nostrils; yet you did not return to me," declares the LORD.*

E. Earthquake (v. 11)

[11] *"I overthrew some of you, as when God overthrew Sodom and Gomorrah, and*

you were as a brand plucked out of the burning; yet you did not return to me,"
declares the LORD.

There is evidence around 763 B.C. that a great earthquake hit the earth.[xlvi] It caught them by surprise and rendered them terrified, but none of this if they saw the warning of a living God.

You may say, "Well, poor old ignorant Amos does not know about secondary causes. It was all about the weather and the barometric pressure, etc." Listen. There is no need to get into an argument about that because Amos is not talking about causes; he is talking about results. He says that when we enter that which impacts our life, it should cause us to stop and ask what our relationship to God is . . . whether it is the barometric pressure or the bear arm of God Himself.

F. Death (v. 12)

[12] *"Therefore thus I will do to you, O Israel; because I will do this to you, prepare to meet your God, O Israel!"*

Notice the words "thus" and "this." It doesn't say "what," it says "thus" and "this." God won't say what He'll do next, but He knows it will amount to this: "Prepare to meet your God, O Israel!" God will not hide behind natural calamities, but He said He will confront Israel and they better prepare to meet God.

Wow! What an implication for our society. The implication is that man in his natural state is not prepared to meet God. If you believe our society believes that, then you probably haven't witnessed to someone in a long time.

Amos informs us that man *must* prepare for a meeting with God. Man *can* prepare for a meeting with God.

III. Cling to God Through Praise No Matter What Happens in Life (v. 13)

This final verse of chapter four is a strange thing. After such a strong word, Amos proclaims a doxology—a word of praise. Amos could praise God for His grace. He could also praise God for His judgment; and that he does.

He informs this generation of proud Israelites, in their urbanity, in their affluence, in their security, that they are not dealing with some totem pole god like Baal of the Phoenicians.

Amos 5:13 says, *13 For behold, he who forms the mountains and creates the wind, and declares to man what is his thought, who makes the morning darkness, and treads on the heights of the earth—the LORD, the God of hosts, is his name!*

A. Praise God for His Creation

The word "forms" (*yôṣēr hārîm*) in this verse is the same word used of a potter playing with clay. God bears that relation to the mountains.[xlvii]

Our God that creates the wind, the great Hebrew word *"bōrē' rûaḥ"*, makes the wind out of nothing.[xlviii]

B. Praise God for His Revelation

He is the God who creates the morning darkness. Amos has in mind the eerie frontal thunderstorm that would loom ominously on the eastern horizon after the sun had risen. He saw on that the hand of God.

The God who is speaking to you is the God who has an arsenal full of weapons to bring you to Him by grace, or if necessary, by judgment.

When God speaks, the high mountains tremble. When God speaks, the sea billows roll. When God speaks, my heart falls to listen. And when God speaks, there is quiet in my soul.[xlix]

Amos would say with the words of that song, "Speak to my heart. Lord, speak to my heart. Lord of creation and God of salvation, speak to my heart today." He forms the mountains. He creates the wind. He says, "Prepare to meet me."

5 | WHAT DOES THE BIBLE SAY ABOUT JUSTICE?

Amos 5

This fifth chapter, right in the heart of the minor prophet book of Amos, is the theme chapter to this book. Amos cries out, finally, in Amos 5:24, *But let justice roll down like waters, and righteousness like an ever-flowing stream.*

George Bernard Shaw, certainly not a Christian, has reminded us that a man's creed is not what he says, but it is the assumption upon which he habitually acts.[1] Shaw the agnostic mirrors the words of Amos the Prophet, that it is not what a generation says, but what a generation does that reveals its real faith. Amos called the hand of the capitol city of the northern kingdom in the eighth century before

Christ.

We have so much in common with them:

- They were urban, and we are urbanized man.
- They were affluent, and we have become affluent man.
- They were religious, and we know the apex of organized religion in terms of statistics and wealth.
- The city to which Amos prophesied just barely saw the light of its bicentennial when judgment came, and we just celebrated our country's 242nd birthday. Amos was prophesying to a young nation, 200 years old, warned of imminent judgment if there was not repentance at the establishment of justice.

Amos was not an eleventh hour prophet; he was a twelfth hour prophet to his generation. He did not hold out hope. He told his generation, "Brace yourself! Judgment is coming," he simply interpreted to them. For us, Amos may be far more redemptive. There is still a time and a chance where we could give heed to the warning of Amos so that the history of his generation in Israel might not also become the history of our generation.

I. The Indictment When Justice is Instructed

Amos addresses the urban and affluent capitol city directly and forcefully. Again and again in the prophecy, like an anvil being struck with a hammer, the word rings out, "justice and righteousness."

In verse 7, Amos levees this indictment, *O you who turn justice to wormwood and cast down righteousness to the earth!* "Justice" is one of the great words of the Prophet Amos. The Hebrew word, *mishpah*, refers to the justice in that society which was to have been dispensed by the civil and legal authorities: to the poor, to the deprived, to the disenfranchised, to the needy, and to the dispossessed. By that, Amos means "justice."

A word of background always helps in this regard. In that day, in the villages and the cities of the kingdom of the north, at the gates of the city, the elders of the land would sit to debate and weigh matters pertaining to civic, business, and moral righteousness. And the elders, who were the wise men of the city, sitting on the benches at the gate of the wall, rendered their verdicts as they determined what was right and what was wrong. But justice meant more to Amos' society than it does to us.

Our courtrooms are decorated with the blindfold-layden justice, but this is not rooted in the Old Testament tradition. The Old Testament rips off the blindfold and turns lady justice loose to set right that which is wrong.

When Amos indicts his generation and calls down God's judgment, because they no longer practice justice, he doesn't mean that they didn't have courts. He doesn't refer to the fact that they didn't have verdicts of "guilty" or "not guilty." He's not talking about objective, impersonal justice as we know it at all. He's indicting the affluent, urban culture for not making right that which was wrong with the righteous needy, poor, and dispossessed. It is because of that that Amos said they turned justice into wormwood.

Justice was to be sweet, to be wholesome to those who sought redress in their weakness. Wormwood was the bitterest of all the shrubs that grew in Israel. It was so bitter that the fate of those who were in exile or those who were prematurely dying were called "wormwood."

Amos says the very place that should have been sweetness was turned into bitterness. Justice has been turned to wormwood. In the same verse (v. 7), he personifies righteousness as if it were personified on a throne with a scepter and a crown. This is another one of Amos' great words.

The Hebrew word in Amos' prophecy that's translated as "righteousness" means "seeking integrity in every relationship to which a man gives himself." It also speaks of the established and powerful man who will speak up for the dispossessed and poor man.

Amos personifies righteousness and he says it has been trampled in the streets. It is as if it has been dethroned and its crown and scepter taken away, and it was left stranded in the streets of the capitol city. But Amos, unlike the preachers of our day, never put people to sleep with mere generalities. Amos becomes specific in his indictments.

Firstly, when justice is obstructed, there is a perversion of justice in the courts. The general population of the capitol city, Samaria, was in a conspiracy of silence against the injustice that was rampant.

Amos 5:10 says, *They hate him who reproves in the gate, and they abhor him who speaks the truth.* When a man of influence and integrity would stand in a public place to suggest that all was not right, he was the object of vilification and abhorrence by society at large. He was hated by those who entered into a conspiracy of silence. Amos says that they abhor the man that speaks the truth. A sincere and guileless man who says, "This is wrong!" is counted a villain and was perhaps called "a bleeding heart liberal."

The bench, itself, was not against taking a bribe. Amos 5:12, speaking of the judges, says, *For I know how many are your transgressions and how great are your sins—you who afflict the righteous, who take a bribe, and turn aside the needy in the gate.* Amos speaks with bitter irony in verse 13, and says, *Therefore he who is prudent will keep silent in such a time, for it is an evil time.*

The affluent, urban man, who knows that something is rotting in society, will follow the prudent course and will enter the conspiracy of silence. He is enjoying the good life in an affluent society, and he does not want to become the one to rock the boat, and to be questioned by his peers. So, Amos says with a bitter irony, "If you are prudent, you'll keep quiet."

The former President of Fuller Theological Seminary, David Allen Hubbard, spoke of an old Alfred Hitchcock show. A couple was going through a southern town on a side road when suddenly, outlaw-like, a local policeman carined in front of them, and ran them off the road and right into a ditch. As he did that, it caused the axle to break on the couple's car. It was ruined! As the policeman jumped out of the squad car, he began to accuse them of many things that they had not done. Finally, he insisted that a tow truck be called. The tow truck driver charged them with an outlandish fee to pull them into town. And you began to see that the policeman and tow truck driver are involved in a conspiracy. Then, when they get to town, the body shop man and the garage man charges an outlandish fee. The coup de grâce is when they go before the justice of the peace and it turns out that he is involved in this little speed trap town, too. It was a malicious conspiracy.

However, Hitchcock had the last word. The woman, of the couple, pulls a recorder from her purse. They were actually state agents, and they were headed to that little town to investigate their speed traps, and it appears they had the goods on everybody. As one watches this, his sense of injustice, his judicial sentiments comes to the fore, but what Amos was reminding his society and what he speaks to us is that there are millions of people in our world for whom all of life is like that. There are people for whom justice is never to be found and all of life is a conspiracy. This is true for some in our nation and true for billions around the earth. Amos would not have us comfortable with that fact.

A. The Economy Crumbles When Justice is Perverted

Amos 5:11 says, *Therefore because you trample on the poor and you exact taxes of grain from him, you have built houses of hewn stone, but you shall not dwell in them; you have planted pleasant vineyards, but you shall not drink their wine.*

Amos is addressing those in the city who dealt out their land to the poor and the rural, righteous needy. They're driving them from the land, and the ill-gotten grain that they used from that to build palaces of hewn stone while the needy righteous with their unredressed grievances live in houses of crumbling clay and brick. They plant pleasant vineyards on the very land they have extorted from the righteous poor.

For Amos, injustice in society and the perversion of social, economic, and business judgment go hand in hand. Have we taken it as a matter of course in our society that dishonesty is expected in the practice and place of commerce?

Have you ever been ripped off? The first car that I bought was a 1990 Chevy Corsica. I started mowing lawns at the age of 11 to begin saving money to have a car when I was 16. I mowed lawns, and saved money over the five year period. Finally, my 16th birthday was approaching. I began searching the newspaper, and finally found a car. My dad went with me, I test drove it, and gave a little under $2,000 to buy this vehicle. Two days later, the car had a rod thrown in the engine. Apparently the man who owned the vehicle put sawdust in the engine to make it temporarily work, but it was truly broken. I got ripped off! We outrage anyone if we suggest dishonesty is taking place.

The problem in Amos' day is not so much that economics and injustice were extant, it is that this dishonesty had become a matter of course. In our society, we expect nothing else. Amos would have a word about the thousands upon thousands of incidences that would become a defective malignancy eating at the fabric of society.

Dr. Elton Trueblood said we live in a "cut-flower civilization."

A cut-flower civilization may for the moment have some beauty—its technological advances are stirring—but it has been cut off from the source of its life and is inevitably decaying. Already we see the wilting petals and the drooping of the leaves. Our nation is already in a state of advanced degeneration.

What is wrong with ethics in America? A few years ago an edition of *Time* magazine featured this cover story: "What Ever Happened to Ethics?"[li] That same kind of story has been found in virtually every newsmagazine in America.[lii,liii]

What is amazing is that the God of Amos was still on the loose.

B. False Religions Flourish When Justice is Perverted

Amos makes radical distinctions that shocked his congregation. The religion that flourishes during days of injustice confuses seeking the Lord with seeking His sanctuary.

Amos 5:4–5 says, *⁴ For thus says the LORD to the house of Israel: "Seek me and live; ⁵ but do not seek Bethel, and do not enter into Gilgal or cross over to Beersheba; for Gilgal shall surely go into exile, and Bethel shall come to nothing.*

Amos, the clever guy that he was, imitates the preachers of that day. In their best, most eloquent homiletical prowess, they proclaim "Come to Bethel!" People were used to hearing advertisements for their sanctuaries. Amos was among the first mighty men to proclaim that seeking the sanctuary is not to be confused with seeking the Lord of the sanctuary.

In verse 4, when it uses the word "seek," it means "to consult, give oneself to totally throw oneself upon the council of another."[liv]

Amos names their popular shrines. "Do not seek Bethel . . ." that was the big one. That was the place of the old time religion. That was where the patriarchs had stopped.

Then verse 5 says, "and do not seek Gilgal . . ." There is a play in the Hebrew words which is best translated into the English, "Gilgal will go to the gallows." Their place of worship will be judged along with them.

Furthermore, in verse 5, it teaches to not "cross over into Beersheba." That place was a great religious retreat the next state over. They went to Beersheba for festivals. Amos just wanted them to be done with all of it.

Seeking the Lord is not to be equated with seeking His sanctuary.

Amos spells-out in verse 4 what its like to seek God in concrete terms. For thus says the LORD to the house of Israel: 'Seek me and live.'" God was saying to them, "Don't litter my sanctuaries with your empty religious processes. Seek to overcome the injustice that is present in the streets and do something about it."

II. Unjust People Do Not Understand the Second-Coming of Christ

Amos 5:18 says, *Woe to you who desire the day of the LORD! Why would you have the day of the LORD? It is darkness, and not light.*

Amos probably spoke this prophetic oracle at the great harvest festival of the fall.[lv] Vintage was in the air. The grapevine, the very symbol of Israel, had once again been triumphantly collected, and the wine vats were full. There was a religious fever nearing hysteria as they sang the song of God's soon-coming intervention against their enemies. Meanwhile, they didn't know that their society had become God's chief enemy. They looked forward to the day of the Lord.

Amos jumps up in the midst of it and says "That day will be darkness for you; not light." There are some today who advise us to live in an eschatological hysteria. They would see our whole orientation should be the capitulation to this age, and an orientation to a return to the Lord.

May He come quickly, but if we just lustily sing, "What a wonderful day, Jesus comes again" and we do not make His priorities for life and society ours, then we might face the shock that Amos suggested.

Our Lord communicated that His intervention would be a delight for those whose priorities were His priorities. The religion that flourishes in days of injustice misunderstands what is acceptable worship.

In verses 21–23, the God of Amos ransacks their religion. He destroys their temple, their feast, and their song.

Amos 5:21–23 says, *21 "I hate, I despise your feasts, and I take no delight in your solemn assemblies. 22 Even though you offer me your burnt offerings and grain offerings, I will not accept them; and the peace offerings of your fattened animals, I will not look upon them. 23 Take away from me the noise of your songs; to the melody of your harps I will not listen.*

As they gathered for Passover and for tabernacles, it had become odious to God. God said, in verse 22, that He would not accept burnt offerings. The elaborate, Levitical, sacrificial system, had been voided of any meaning to the Living God who saw injustice and perversion of life.

Even their songs were religious and not worshipful. God despises disingenuous musical worship. Note what verse 23 says, *Take away from me the noise of your songs.* What they thought was harmony was truly a cacophony on the ears of the Living God. Stern words? Yes. But they were true.

The worship of people who are given to a lifestyle of injustice is dismissed with the wave of a hand. What does God want? Is He an exacting and demanding God?

The key verse in this entire chapter is verse 24, *But let justice roll down like waters, and righteousness like an ever-flowing stream.* As a shepherd, Amos had grown used to the deceitful brooks of Palestine called "woddies." Now and then, they were filled with water. Sadly, all too often, there is a deceitful promise of water that is, in actuality, nowhere to be found.

Amos dreamed of a land where streams were flowing and justice was rolling. He dreamed of righteousness, integrity, in every relation between man and man, and man and woman, would flow on unobstructed. That was the pinnacle of Amos' vision. And he said that until that is our vision, the sanctuary doesn't mean that much to the Lord.

III. There is Finality to This Prophecy

Amos, never a bore, jumped up to say in the first verse of this chapter, "I have an obituary!" and everyone's ears perked up to see who died.

Amos 5:1–2a says, *¹Hear this word that I take up over you in lamentation, O house of Israel: ² "Fallen, no more to rise, is the virgin Israel;* He compares Israel to a young lady in the prime of health and the vibrancy of life who then fell into an irretrievable and irremedial death.

Amos 5:2b–3 says, *forsaken on her land, with none to raise her up.' ³ For thus says the Lord GOD: 'The city that went out a thousand shall have a hundred left, and that which went out a hundred shall have ten left to the house of Israel.'*

It's a picture of military disaster. Amos looks at their districts of conscription, their selective service centers, and a city that sent 1,000 into a coming battle. They'll see 100 struggle to come back. Then, the city that sees one hundred will see ten wind their way back. The nation that is enthroned in injustice will face a devastating military catastrophe that will leave only $1/10^{th}$ of their troops intact.

Amos spoke these words in the midst of the eighth century, and within three decades, under the leadership of Tiglath Pilesar, his words had literally, statistically, historically, actually, come to pass. That's why we still have his prophecy. If it had not come to fruition, it would have been discarded.

Again, look at Amos 5:2a, *Fallen, no more to rise, is the virgin Israel.* This was not a very pretty picture. Amos had to tell his generation, "Brace yourself; it's the twelfth hour. Nothing can be done." There is a terrible finality in his word "the virgin Israel has fallen." Thankfully, it wasn't God's last word in the world.

There was another word of prophecy. Matthew 1:23 says, *Behold, the virgin shall conceive and bear a son, and they shall call his name Immanuel.*

When hope was lost and failure looked final in the darkest hour, God brought about the birth of that one in whom mercy and justice would meet. This was the one who Amos only dimly, if ever, foresaw. This one, Jesus, guarantees to us the Spirit so we can live a life of justice and a life of integrity.

We do not point to the virgin of Israel falling in the dust of history; we point to the one conceived of a virgin who on Calvary showed us what justice and mercy is all about. So, it is not to the funeral dirge of Amos that I invite you to come to Christ right now. But it is to that one conceived of a virgin and crucified on Calvary, and vindicated by God's justice in a resurrection. This was a greater hope . . . that we might know life and justice and mercy, and what it is to walk humbly before God.

6 | A WAKE UP CALL FROM GOD TO YOU

Amos 6

Amos spoke in the sixth chapter of his prophecy and he still speaks today. Godless humanism has loosened the spiritual fiber of the west. A minor league baseball team in Saint Paul, MN, the Saint Paul Saints, planned an "atheist night" where they rewarded a belief in no god with free entry to their stadium. Furthermore, they are changed the name of their team's mascot for one game from the "Saints" to the "Aints."[lvi]

We must roar out like Amos against civic cowardice. We must roar against irresponsible and licentious press. If you do this, you will be a rare person. If you stand up for God, you will be different. However, you will be like the prophet Amos.

We could become like a society, thinking for a moment that we are resting in the snow only to find its sleep will last forever. Amos never tired of certain themes, and he never broke his hammer striking these themes. I suppose that the largest of his themes was that of an urban society built at the expense of an oppressed lower class.

He also spoke of those with an over-weaning sense of pride, grounded in a supposed military superiority. He spoke to an undisciplined people. He spoke of injustice and the impending judgment of God through it all.

Laced together in my thinking of Amos, comes back to a belief in an erroneous worldview that became the basis for government and social science. This could be defined as rationalistic humanism or humanistic autonomy. The proclaimed and enforced autonomy of man from any higher force above him, if based in modern western civilization of man and his modern material needs.

However, in early democracies, including the American democracy at the time of its birth, all individual rights were granted as God's creature.[lvii] Over time, man's sense of responsibility to God and society grew dimmer and dimmer.

Dr. Rufus Spain, a professor at Baylor University, wrote a book entitled *At Ease in Zion*.[lviii] When I first came across this book, I thought he had come up with a very clever title. Only several years later did I learn that he borrowed it from Amos. He was suggesting that maybe we have a word to hear from the ancient prophet.

What are some of the signs when we are at ease in Zion?

I. They Misplaced Their Faith

In this sixth chapter, Amos is addressing his words to the self-proclaimed chief men of the capitol city of the nation, the city of Samaria. Here, there had developed an ever-expanding democracy that was supported by the exploitation of the small, rural villages filled with farmers that were gradually being forced out of their place by the ever-expanding urban centers. By their own estimate, Amos was addressing the first men of the nation. In the first verse he addresses those known as the "first of the nations."

Amos 6:1 says, *Woe to those who are at ease in Zion, and to those who feel secure on the mountain of Samaria, the notable men of the first of the nations, to whom the house of Israel comes!*

They, with their over-weaning pride, in the mushrooming prosperity of that urban center suddenly gone wild, considered themselves to be the very first of the first.

The Hebrew word for "at ease," שַׁאֲנַן, is a word that speaks of a reckless optimism.[lix] It is a facile trust that everything is copacetic. It is a groundless sense of security.

One can almost hear them sing, "Home, home in Samaria. Where the Jew and the Israelite play. Where seldom is heard a discouraging word and the Torah is read every day."

II. They Worshiped Structures, Not God

Amos further describes them as those who give their religious trust not to the god of their history, but to the structures of their capitol city. They habitually trust the mountain of Samaria. 40 times in the Old Testament, that word for trust, "בָּטַח" is used of the trust that belongs to God alone.[lx] They lost track of God and began to believe that they were the authors of their own history and not the almighty God. So, they deposit the confidence that belongs to Him not in the unseen God that took a slave nation and forces them into Israel, but into the political machinations of the capitol city, built with their own hands.

It may be one of the benedictions of our generation that this seems to be less of a temptation. It seems that we're coming around to see that we need a higher security than that which is social. We need more care than Medicare. We need a higher court of justice than the highest court in the land. But Amos' generation deposited the trust that belonged to God alone and placed it in their own hands.

This was reflected in unmitigated bragging. Amos quotes them in verse 2. It is almost as if the chamber of commerce of Samaria was leading a world tour. Amos 6:2 says, *Pass over to Calneh, and see, and from there go to Hamath the great; then go down to Gath of the Philistines. Are you better than these kingdoms? Or is their territory greater than your territory,*

Now, those are not every day places. Calneh was a prosperous kingdom in northern Syria that had vanished.[lxi] Hamith was an independent kingdom, north of Israel, that had fallen on hard times.[lxii] And the Philistines, formerly of Old Testament might, were now facing substantial weaning of their power.[lxiii] The over-weaning pride of the courtiers of the king in Samaria say "Look at these! For such an hour as this, we have grasped our manifest destiny! Our history and our future is in our hand."

How quickly they had forgotten that five centuries before when God had been the author of history of an impoverished slave people. Like the rich man who built bigger barns, they considered that destiny was in their hands.

If there had been some Jonathan Swift, he would have written of the Lilliputian little people who thought they had tied down God with what was, in reality, pieces of string.[lxiv] The citizens of northern Israel would find, like Gullivar would later discover, what would rise up and snap the chords that bound him.

They suffered from what Soren Kierkegaard called "sickness unto death," namely the feeling that there are infinite possibilities for man, even apart from God.[lxv]

III. The Leadership was Extremely Luxurious and Indifferent

There is evidence that even Amos' generation sensed something was wrong. In Amos 6:3, he indicts them by saying, *O you who put far away the day of disaster and bring near the seat of violence?* Looking beyond the next bend in the road, beyond the next page on the turn of a calendar, even the affluent generation of the capitol city of Samaria sensed that there was reckoning. The existentialists that they were, not willing to admit that the essence of life was responsibility before God, Amos says that they pushed away the evil day that lurked before them, around the corner of the destiny of the nation.

Instead of that, he says, they enthrone violence and injustice. To meet the needs of the moment, they continue a life of brutish and animalistic insensitivity and exploitation of the capitol city of the nation.

Amos goes on next to give us a vignette, a cameo, a little picture of what life was like in the capitol city of Samaria. There's nothing else like this in all of the prophets. Amos describes in detail a panorama of life that has given itself to insensitivity and luxury until it has tenderized the moral muscle of the nation.

He says, in Amos 6:4a, *Woe to those who lie on beds of ivory....* In 1943, an archaeological expedition in Samaria found chips of this very ivory that Amos mentions here.[lxvi]

Amos 6:4b says, *and stretch themselves out on their couches.* The Hebrew, *sĕruḥîm*, suggests that they "sprawled out." This word was used historically to represent tapestries as they hung loosely from the window.[lxvii] The Hebrews practiced sitting up in chairs and dining until a foreign influence led them to lull themselves out, be numb with Bacchanalian banquets, they sprawl out over their couches.[lxviii]

Further, in Amos 6:4, it says they would *eat lambs from the flock.* Only the most choice veal would do for them. In a society where the poor would only eat meat once per week, they would take lambs from the flock. There is some sadness in this. The Hebrews were historically a pastoral people.[lxix] They had not eaten veal; they had been shepherds. The little lambs had provided fleece and milk, but now, in the "gotta have it now" generation, they took the lambs out of the flock and the calves out of the feeding lodge, and while they're doing this, they chant to the sound of a stringed instrument.

Amos 6:5 says, *⁵ who sing idle songs to the sound of the harp and like David invent for themselves instruments of music, ⁶ who drink wine in bowls and anoint themselves with the finest oils, but are not grieved over the ruin of Joseph!*

They invented musical instruments, just like David. Every man thought that he was a little David. It means, "to extemporize music spontaneously."[lxx] In their boredom, in their aimless sprawl across their couches, they extemporized songs. The word suggests a howl, or a screech.[lxxi] They imagined they were little Davids.

Our country, that has been stupefied by television, obsession with cell phones, and intolerable music, can relate to these Hebrews engaged in a similar lifestyle.

Amos 6:6a says, [6] *who drink wine in bowls.*

You see, goblets were no longer sufficient for all of the booze they were drinking. Bowls were often used for the sacred vessels in the temple, and even they may have been appropriated for the "gotta have it now" generation that lived in Samaria.

Amos 6:6b says they, *anoint themselves with the finest oils,*

The common man would put olive oil on his skin to protect him from the sun and the drying wind. Some would put spices in them. It was the Old Testament version of Chanel no. 5.

These people were eating, drinking, and having a big party. You might say, "Well, what's wrong with a good steak every now and then?" Nothing. There are no two things on this list given by the prophet Amos that would indicate a life in sin against God. However, Amos draws a picture of one thing after another that piles up for us to see a society that in all of its activities had become brutish and animalistic. Amos is describing that these people were living their lives for their own luxury and only thinking about the immediate moment of their own pleasure. This is the definition of hedonism.

The irony is that they are not grieved for the wound of Joseph. Amos' voice trails-off in verse 6. They are not grieved for Joseph. Joseph's name is being used as a representation of the people of Israel. While they lived in a vortex of pleasure, their society was wounded. It wreaks with open sores of injustice while they extemporize about how great they are.

Sometimes, we need to be shocked by a word from someone like Amos about the dangers of unbridled affluence. We're an affluent people. God has been good to us. We can remain God's people if it is always with an irritated sensitivity to the dangers that lurk in a life of affluence. Paul said he knew how to abase and he knew how to abound, and by that Paul meant to not follow the sound of affluence everywhere it went.

Affluence does not give you joy. It has the propensity to give you temporal happiness, but only Jesus gives joy. That's because joy is everlasting and happiness is temporal. Think of the multitude of millionaires plagued by sadness: Lindsay Lohan, Elvis Presley, Kurt Cobain, etc.

Amos has spoken of their pride, but he continues by speaking of the judgment upon those who are at ease in Zion. These people were in such a rush in life, and they always wanted to be first. They'll now have the opportunity to be first in everything.

Look at Amos 6:7, *Therefore they shall now be the first of those who go into exile.*

For those who wanted to be first at any price, what they were doing simply served as a dress rehearsal for their journey as the first into exile. The end of verse 7 is oh so poetic, *and the revelry of those who stretch themselves out shall pass away.* This means "the spree of the sprawlers will be ended."[lxxii]

Then, there comes what I would consider the weirdest scene in all of the book of Amos.

Amos 6:9–10 says, [9] *And if ten men remain in one house, they shall die.* [10] *And when one's relative, the one who anoints him for burial, shall take him up to bring the bones out of the house, and shall say to him who is in the innermost parts of the house, "Is there still anyone with you?" he shall say, "No"; and he shall say, "Silence! We must not mention the name of the LORD.*

It's like going into the twilight zone. Amos pictures the city of Samaria, after the predicted decimation, every chapter of Amos after the first speaks of God's judgment as a military victory over Israel.

- Chapter two speaks of flight perishing from the swift.
- Chapter three speaks of the only evidence remaining will be the kind of evidence left when a lion is finished with a lamb.
- Chapter four warns them in similar tones.

- Chapter five says the vineyard will become the place of sorrow.
- This theme in Amos reaches a crescendo in the sixth chapter.

In another cameo, he pictures a man's kinsman going to the home of his former family. In the decimation of a military victory and in the plague that follows, he is there to do his last duties to his kinspeople in verse 10. He is going about these duties in a very makab, eery and grotesque manner. Then, in a whisper, he asks if there is anyone else in the house. From the innermost recesses of the house, there comes a word—HUSH—do not speak the name of the Lord.

In one day, God's name has been written lamely over their society and has been taken lightly on their lips. Suddenly, this becomes a very serious matter to them. As a man surviving in the back of the house uses the very word that was used in the temple services—HUSH—silence before God. Do not even speak His name. We know his reality now.

Sometimes people will ask me if I believe our nation is beyond the tipping point of taking God seriously again. Will it take decades? Will it take centuries? If I understand the God of Amos, He is the God who within a day's time, if necessary, can bring people to reverence His name. It is out of mercy and grace that He forestalls that day.

We need not think that the judge of all the earth is without resources that man should take his name with seriousness. Amos describes the hush that fell across Samaria. They said, "Don't speak His name unless you speak it vainly."

Helmet Thieleke describes those days when judgment was falling on the Nazi regime on the third reich, and when he went to stand in his church, in the smoldering ruins of that church, holding only the key to it in his hand with the rest of it gone. He said that he stood there in smoke and ruin in paratroop boots when he and his flock were overcome with the reality of God as both just and gracious.[lxxiii]

IV. They Made Odds with God

Amos mentions two absurdities. In verse 12, he says, *Do horses run on rocks? Does one plow there with oxen? But you have turned justice into poison and the fruit of righteousness into wormwood.*

The two absurdities mentioned here are : (1) They had their horses in Palestine, but when they used them, they would not run them. The ground was too rocky. Their hooves would split, and they would be ruined. (2) To make the absurdity even greater, he mentions that they would not plow their oxen into the Mediterranean.

He says that a people who would not dare act with absurdity in the physical world have acted with absurdity in the spiritual world. So, he says, they have turned justice, *mishpah*, God's desire to make things right, and they turned it into poison. They turned righteousness into wormwood (which, as we discussed before, represents bitterness). They tried to turn the moral world upside down and said, "We will not fall off." It is absurd to try to make odds with God.

We're a gambling generation. I recently read about a machine in Las Vegas called "Big Bertha."[lxxiv] Now, I haven't played it, so don't quote me. It has eight rows of digits all the way across, and the only way you can win is if you have all eight rows aligned with acorns, or hearts, or whatever shows up. The odds are insurmountable, but I read that people stay there day and night, pumping dollars into the motion with hope that they'll beat the odds.

Amos' generation thought they could play the odds against God, and beat the moral and spiritual odds against a nation that places its trust that lives in an insensitive luxury, and thinks that it will forestall the judgment of God.

Conclusion

May I never leave the book of Amos without saying "Thank God this is not the last word." I do not always sense the compassion in Amos that I would like to see in him. Amos was an angry man. I have to turn to another man in another capitol. You see, our Lord Jesus Christ took the injustice of the city of Jerusalem onto Himself, and in that matchless recycling that we call "the resurrection" turned injustice into God's greatest moment of justice.

Thank the Lord that the Bible does not conclude with a smoking city in smoldering ruins. It ends with God's grace of a new Jerusalem, coming down out of heaven, not for the judgment of the nations, but for the healing of the nations. Our invitation is to our ultimate destiny, heaven. The city has a builder and the builder is God. That's the good news of the Bible, beyond what Amos could ever see. And this is my invitation to you day. Come to Jesus.

7 | PRAYER IN THE MIDST OF CRISIS

Amos 7

In 1863, President Lincoln called for national humiliation and prayer, "We have been the recipients of the choicest bounties of heaven. We have been preserved these many years in peace. We have grown in prosperity and wealth and numbers as no other country has ever grown, but we have forgotten God. We have forgotten the gracious hand that preserved us in peace, and multiplied and enriched and strengthened us, and we have vainly imagined in the deceitfulness of our hearts that all of these blessings were produced by some superior wisdom virtue of our own. Intoxicated in all of our own success, we have become too self-sufficient to feel the necessity of redeeming."[lxxv]

Can you imagine an American president preaching that we have been too proud to thank the God who made us? It behooves us to repent and confess our national sense and beg for clemency and forgiveness.

In the seventh chapter of Amos, we learn that for Christians, the distinctive contribution you must have is that you plead before God for the nation in which we live.

Amos was a layman whose occupation was keeping sheep, raven jet-black-haired sheep, and pitching the sycamore fruit in order to help it ripen. Yet, while he was doing that, he had a vision. That vision was of the future destiny of the nation unless he prayed and God intervened.

It would behoove each and every one of us that the distinctive contribution each of us could make as followers of Christ and American citizens is to plead with God for our nation.

How do we pray for our nation?

This text contains four visions. Two of these visions speak of a potential future. Amos asked God to prohibit, avert, deflect, postpone that future, and God did. The latter two visions, the visions of the plumb line and of ripened fruit brought no such response from God. God said, "Too late. I'll not pass by any more."

How should we pray for our nation?

I. Pray When Your Perspective Becomes Different

Amos, this layman from Tekoa who lived in isolation, was a seer. The very Hebrew word for "prophet" means "seer." This rural, rustic, bucolic, sheep-keeping, sycamore-fruit-pitching layman from Tekoa, as unlikely of a person as you could find, had a vision. He saw what others could not see.

If we pray intensely, it is because we feel deeply, and if we feel deeply it is because we see clearly. What did he see? He had a vision. That vision was one of agricultural disaster in an agrarian land.

Amos 7:1–3 says, *¹ This is what the Lord GOD showed me: behold, he was forming locusts when the latter growth was just*

> *beginning to sprout, and behold, it was the latter growth after the king's mowings. ² When they had finished eating the grass of the land, I said, "O Lord GOD, please forgive! How can Jacob stand? He is so small!" ³ The LORD relented concerning this: "It shall not be," said the LORD.*

Again, look at verse 1, *This is what the Lord GOD showed me: behold, he was forming locusts…* Literally, the Hebrew means "the larval form of a locust." The first verse goes on to say, *…when the latter growth was just beginning to sprout, and behold, it was the latter growth after the king's mowings.* What did he see? His seeing didn't exclude the auditory. He also heard it. Like a great swarm of locusts coming. There he was with the sheep bleeding, sycamore trees growing, and Amos sees what others could not see. We see the coming of a locust invasion.

You and I cannot imagine what a disaster that was.[lxxvi] When he saw them in a larval stage, he saw the insipient beginning of what was going to happen unless God intervened. That is, every leaf stripped from every tree. That means every grain stripped from every stalk. Every piece of fruit stripped from every vine. In that agricultural nation it would have been a disaster.

We read some modern descriptions of them in 1865, 1870, 1890, 1892, 1904, and most of all in 1915 there was such a locust plague in the Holy Land. In 1915, when reading accounts of it, the plague was heard before it was seen.[lxxvii] The people heard it coming, and then they saw it like an eclipse of the sun. Those who wrote about the 1915 locust plague said it blackened the sky like it was an eclipse, like it was midnight. They said everywhere they looked they saw the excrement of locusts and every man between 16 and 60 was commanded to pick-up a dozen pounds of locust eggs every day and throw them into the sea to try to avert the disaster. It was a calamity.

Amos, who was able to see what others could not see, saw a potential future for the nation. He saw a locust plague, but then he looked again, and he had another vision.

Amos 7:4–6, *⁴ This is what the Lord GOD showed me: behold, the Lord GOD was calling for a judgment by fire, and it devoured the great deep and was eating up the land. ⁵ Then I said, "O Lord GOD, please cease! How can Jacob stand? He is so small!" ⁶ The LORD relented concerning this: "This also shall not be," said the Lord GOD.*

This sheep-keeping Tekoan saw a fire. It may have been a natural fire. It may have been a brush fire. Spontaneous combustion. That fire was just devouring, like a panzer division, the scrub brush on the desert floor around Tekoa.[lxxviii]

It may have been supernatural fire. That is what is suggested because it devoured the great deep. This fire reached down into the subterranean sources of water that fed the springs that nurtured Israel, and he saw a doubling of the disaster because after the entire agricultural crop had been destroyed, it would've been oblivion for all of the water to disappear. He saw that potential future.

This leads me to ask you as Christians, do you see anything differently from how others see things? How do you look at things? Do you see with a sense of "me-ism"? This indifference typifies many in the generations living today. Do you look at things with scorn in the face of possible disintegration? Do you look at things with nearsightedness by saying, "As long as my family and I are OK, I'm not going to worry about it."

Do you look at things like Ruth Bell Graham, who quipped one time what has been taken more seriously in recent years and that is, "If God doesn't judge America, He owes Sodom and Gomorrah an apology."[lxxix] Why should we think that we are an exception?

Robert Bellah, a secular writer, using four researchers, said that our nation is in the grip of an individualistic ethic, a selfish lifestyle that is eroding community, and will end our destiny.[lxxx] If you think not, look at some decisions made by our country's leadership: In 1973, the Supreme Court decided abortion was legal; in 1989 prayer before high school ball games was illegal; and in 2015 the Supreme Court decided gay marriage should be legalized. If anything, we are to see what others cannot see.

We need to recognize that if we are to be like Amos and pray for our nation, we must see things others do not see even when they're not pleasant.

II. Pray When Crisis Comes

This locust plague stripped every leaf from every tree, all the bark from every bush, it took all the grain and fruit, and the fire would have devoured the deep. It was a matter of pleading with God at the critical moment.

That is pointed to in this strange expression in verse 1: *it was the latter growth after the king's mowings.* Now, that would mean nothing. It would have been an ancient, boring detail if we didn't look into it with greater insight. In Amos' world, the king got the first harvest.[lxxxi] Jeroboam got it all. The general population was dependent upon the second harvest after the April rains after which there was six months of drought and no more grain.

That is, it was at just the critical moment that Amos had his vision and prayed his prayer. Had this layman not intervened at just that critical moment, it would have been too late.

Very practically, we must learn to pray for our nation just as Amos prayed for his nation. You may say, "Well, how do I pray for my country?" Look at verse 2, then at verse 5. Having seen clearly, he felt deeply. Having felt deeply, he prayed intensely—not lengthily, but intensely.

Look at the attitude of this prayer: *² I said, "O Lord GOD." ⁵ Then I said, "O Lord GOD."*

If there is anybody who is serious about asking God for national destiny, how do you address him? With reverence and relationship. Look at the reverence.

A. Reverence in Prayer

The very word means "sovereign Lord!" It is an acknowledgement that the destiny of our nation is in His hands, not out of His hands.

When we pray to God, we are dealing with the very same sovereign, heavenly, imperial potentate who has already dealt with Pharaoh—that's ancient history. He's already dealt with Nebuchadnezzar—that's 2,600 years ago. He's already dealt with Hitler, Lenin, Stalin, Hussein, and Bin Ladin. When we bow to Him, we're bowing to the One in whose hands the destiny of the nations rest and you say to Him, "Oh sovereign God!"

B. Relationship in Prayer

The Hebrew, אֲדֹנָי יְהוִה, literally says, "Oh my Lord God."[lxxxii] When Amos prayed, he prayed out of a relationship with the God to whom he was speaking. In anticipation Jesus cried, "Abba, Father!" That's the way we pray for anything or anybody. It's the tension.

We come recognizing the exalted character of God. He's omnipotent and I am powerless, He is exalted and I am minute and time-bound and dying. But on the other hand, I come out of a sense of relationship to Him where I can say, "Oh, Abba . . . my God." We must recognize that He is sovereign, but also note that we can go to Him with an uninterrupted personal relationship.

You may say, "Well, what is the pith, the center, the marrow of it? How do you pray?" This prayer is brief. It is incredibly brief as it is recorded here.

When he had the vision of the locusts, look at his prayer. The intercession is really one word: FORGIVE! He couldn't plead national repentance because they hadn't repented. He couldn't say there was a revival, forgive them, he didn't. This one word (סְלַח) means to forgive by cleansing. In the matter of the fire that would have devoured, it was even brief.

In the middle of verse 5, Amos cries, "O Lord GOD, please cease!" He couldn't say "forgive." He couldn't say, "They have repented." With intensity, that shepherd at Tekoa cried out to the throne of God, "Cease! Postpone! Wait!" Jesus raised Lazarus with three words in the English Bible, "Lazarus, come forth." This leads me to think that God is not so much interested in the length or composition or liturgy or eloquence or order of the way we pray than when we look out and see clearly, and feel deeply, and pray intensely, then we can say, "Oh God, CEASE! Give us another chance."

What was his appeal to God? Well, like I said, it wasn't like anyone repented because they hadn't. It wasn't that Israel deserved it because they didn't. He repeatedly says to forgive. Both times, he gives the same reason (in v. 2 and v. 5), "How can Jacob stand? He is small." I look at this and think about how to pray for the United States. How do you pray in the face of secularism and hedonism? How do you pray when entire university campuses have been given over to hollow men with anti-Christian agendas. How do you pray?

Here's how you pray to God. I need to know it, and you do, too. He prayed to God to have mercy on them because they were so small. Look at their hopelessness. Look at their helplessness. If God didn't intervene, could these Israelites ever recover? Amos was crying out to God that since He is compassionate and merciful, He wants God to reach out and cease.

How do you pray for a nation? You pray like that. You may be thinking, "Well, our country is not small." You know what? In a sense, you're right. America is the third-largest country in land mass, and the third-largest country in population. We have the greatest military power in the world. Despite this, we're no match for the almighty God.

The idea is absurd to say that we stand in the face of what God can do. What we, as Americans, must say is, "Oh God, please cease, postpone! In light of Your throne, we are so small."

If you don't believe that, go ask Pharaoh. He was leader of the most powerful empire up to that time. He got into a duel with Jehovah and found that finite people always lose.

It is interesting that he called Israel by the name "Jacob." He didn't generalize, he particularized. I don't know about you, but it is very hard for me to pray for huge millions of people.

I once thought about it when I was circling over the Newark, NJ airport, and we flew around the Statue of Liberty a few times, waiting for our turn to land. I was thinking of the 8.2 million people who live in that one city.

Those people looked like little ants walking around, and I began wondering what it would be like if God would save all of those people. However, I also wondered what it would be like if God judged all of them. I've done the same thing looking out over London and Chicago and Miami, but it is hard to generalize. That's why here, Amos used the single name, "Jacob." He said that he could not think about all of Israel.

It is abstract and generalized for a preacher to get up and say, "What if God judged all of America or all of Greenville?" But it is different if I ask myself, "What if the judgment of God came on this nation, and it fell on Bob or Sue, or Wes, or my mom, or my good friend?" And the individuals I knew were caught up in national confrontation with God.

You may think, "Well, the whole nation is too big for me to pray for it." Well, at least do what Amos did and hold up those nearest and dearest to you. Just say, "Oh God, please postpone, wait, forgive."

How did God respond? Well, God can relent. And in this instance, God did. Amos, this seer, saw judgment. He prayed briefly and intensely.

Verse 3 says, *The LORD relented concerning this: "It shall not be," said the LORD.* Other versions say the Lord "repented" of this. When He saw the firestorm, and interceded, in verse 6, He relented again.

What does that mean? You always get in trouble when you try to be more biblical than the Bible. The Hebrew, אָמַר, word means "groan, sigh, change of mind."[lxxxiii]

One of the basic differences between liberal Protestantism in America and conservative, evangelical, fundamental Christianity is this: Liberal Protestantism says that if I pray, God will change me and I'll feel better about the way things are. But conservative, biblical Christianity says one praying layman at Tekoa can call out to the throne of God and not just change Amos, but change the direction of his nation. Personal faith rises or falls with that kind of understanding.

God relented in the face of the prayers of Amos. Do you remember the story of Abraham in Genesis 18? He was bargaining with God about whether or not He would judge Sodom and Gomorrah. This was an incredible give-and-take between Abraham and Jehovah. Abraham said, "If there are 50 people who are right with you, will you destroy them?" And God said, "No." It was like a bargaining session with God. What if there are 45 or 40? What if there are 20? What if there are 10?

This means that God is not a computer spitting out impersonal faith. He didn't wind this world up like a clock, then just walk away from it. It means that God's people can make a difference in national destiny if God's people, like an Amos, see clearly and pray intensely. If we are in any sense biblical Christians, we best believe that He does now.

I hope and pray and plead under the Holy Spirit of God that the people reading this book believe in the power of prayer.

However, there are times when God does not pass. In Amos 7, 8:1–2, Amos saw a plumb line. That plumb line went down a building to make sure it was stable, straight, and square.

Amos 7:7–9 says, *⁷ This is what he showed me: behold, the Lord was standing beside a wall built with a plumb line, with a plumb line in his hand. ⁸ And the* LORD *said to me, "Amos, what do you see?" And I said, "A plumb line." Then the Lord said, "Behold, I am setting a plumb line in the midst of my people Israel; I will never again pass by them; ⁹ the high places of Isaac shall be made desolate, and the sanctuaries of Israel shall be laid waste, and I will rise against the house of Jeroboam with the sword.*

Do you know how long Israel lasted as a nation with ten northern tribes? 922 B.C.–722 B.C. 200 years. Our country is 242 years old.

Our hope is the intercession of God's people. But there is personal hope for you beyond that. Your hope of heaven and eternal life, thank God, doesn't rest on the plumb line being put alongside you. No. One day, on Calvary, God dropped His plumb line along the cross. He measured the life and death of Jesus Christ. God the Father said that Jesus was always square, never out of line, always straight and upright. If you'll trust in Him, no matter what happens to our nation, it will deflect God's judgment on a nation from you.

I can't predict what will happen to our nation, how God's people will pray, whether God will intervene or not, but I can tell you that if you give your life to Jesus Christ, God the Father has measured Him and found Him perfect. When you trust Him and Him alone for salvation, you experience the deflection of God's wrath and the gift of life everlasting.

8 | WAITING FOR MONDAY

Amos 8

To entitle Amos 8, I would want to write over it with the words, "Hurry up with the benediction." This is precisely the sentiment that Amos discovers and that he probes in the eighth and next-to-last chapter of this eighth century prophecy.

For those of us who pursue the precarious, potent profession of preaching publicly, it is often a leisure-time pursuit to wonder what people are thinking about while we're standing up here. One is reminded of the words of Jeremiah 1:17, *Do not be dismayed by them.* And I have seen some dismayed faces over the decade I have been preaching.

Perhaps if we were to be given insight into what echoes inside the skulls of our hearers while our words echo in their ears, it might be a fascination to know what was being thought. Perhaps someone would be thinking, "Why doesn't he get a new suit; he has worn that one twice in the last three weeks." "How does he get his hair to stand up like that?" "I wonder if they leave the water in that baptistery or just drain it every time." "I wonder if Pastor Jeremy can see me when I fall asleep in church." Or the perennial favorite, "I wonder if I left the coffee pot on."

Amos was given that which was denied to us mere mortal preachers. He was given by God insights into the thoughts of his auditors at the national shrine of the northern kingdom Israel: Dan and Bethel. His listeners in the capitol city of Samaria, the x-ray vision of Amos and his keen spiritual perception gave him insight into what they were thinking while they were there at the national shrines of worship in an affluent age. And that which he heard led him to conclude that they were saying, "Hurry up with the benediction."

As I have entitled this message "Waiting for Monday," it speaks of those who are in a house of worship who are calculating, thinking, are involved in planning social injustice in the midst of social tolerance. To this, Amos was called to give a word. Namely, that generation was a terminal generation by the very oath of God Himself. In an age when injustice was rampant, when religion was shallow, Amos said that national judgment was sure.

What is the Word of God to people when their response to Him, even in worship, is "Hurry up with the benediction." When God's people say, "Hurry up with the benediction", there is . . .

I. The Revelation of God's Judgment

We see in this eighth chapter, the medium, message, and motif of God's revelation.

Amos 8:1–2 says, *This is what the Lord GOD showed me: behold, a basket of summer fruit. [2] And he said, "Amos, what do you see?" And I said, "A basket of summer fruit." Then the LORD said to me, "The end has come upon my people Israel; I will never again pass by them."*

Already, Amos had seen the fresh vision of locusts, and God relented of national judgment. Amos had seen that contending of God by fire, and once again when Amos cried out to God for Him to cease, God once again relented of the disaster He said He would do to them. Then, in the third vision, God showed Amos the plumb line, the vision of finality. This vision of summer fruit (the fourth of Amos' visions) is but an application of that vision of God's plumb line laid down besides God's people to show they are out of square with God's purposes.

The time is the fall harvest festival when the fruit was safely gathered together.[lxxxiv] The air is filled with festive ballads. It was the new-year time, the time of beginnings, not the end, the time of renewal, not of ruins. But in the midst of the howling of the ballads and the revelry of the celebration, Amos who stands by quietly ignored fastens his x-ray vision on one basket of the fruit. Caught up in the charisma of prophetic insight, he hears the word of Jehovah.

In Amos 8:2a the Lord says, *"Amos, what do you see?" And I said, "A basket of summer fruit."* And suddenly that basket of ripened fruit becomes the common thing that is the vehicle of Jehovah's revelation. Just like Moses' rod that became the rod of God, just like Elijah's mantle that became the mantle of power, that basket of ripe fruit, as common as it was, becomes the vehicle for God's Word about the fate of a nation.

You see, a prophet is not someone who sees unusual things so much as someone who sees more deeply into very ordinary things. The medium of revelation was a basket of ripe fruit, but what was its message? The message was, "No exit. This is a terminal generation."

There is here in the Hebrew language a subtle play on words. The Hebrew word for "ripened fruit", "כְּלוּב קָיִץ" is a word pronounced "qāyiṣ."[lxxxv] And the Hebrew word for "the end" is a word pronounced "qēṣ".[lxxxvi] What Amos heard can be reproduced in English by saying this, "What do you see, Amos?" "I see a basket of plumbs." "That's right, Amos. You see a basket of plumbs. And Israel will plummet toward its end."

In the assonance of that homonym, that sound-a-like word, Amos saw in that basket of fruit a word about the end. When everyone else at the harvest festival said it is the beginning, it is the burden of Amos who said it was the end. When everyone else was saying it was a time of renewal, it was the burden of Amos to say it was the time of ruin.

Like those who are partying on the upper-deck of a luxury liner, after a fatal leak has sprung beneath the water line, Amos' generation was in no mood. But Amos, more than any other prophet in the Old

Testament, spoke a word about "no exit" to an affluent generation who said, "Hurry up with the benediction." This message came by the motif of ripened fruit. The motif is a sudden reversal of their society.

Amos 8:3 says, *The songs of the temple shall become wailings in that day,"* *declares the Lord GOD. "So many dead bodies!" "They are thrown everywhere!"* *"Silence!"*

This is a motif of reversal. The songstresses of the temple, who sang at national holidays, whose festival ballads were ringing in the ears of the holiday celebrants in Bethel were prized as a treasure by the king as much as his gold or his silver. The songs of the songstresses were to be reversed to the sadness of funeral dirges.

When a society becomes thoroughly secular and irreversibly materialistic, it is already under God's terminal judgment. All Amos could say to those folks who were trying to hurry up the benediction was "hush."

Max Lucado wrote a book entitled *God's Story, Your Story: When His Becomes Yours.*[lxxxvii] In his book, he writes:

But then the flies come out. People die, earthquakes rumble, and nations rage. Families collapse, and children die of hunger. Dictators snort and treat people like, well, like pigs. And this world stinks. And we have a choice. We can pretend this life is all God intended. Or . . . We can come to our senses. We can follow the example of the prodigal son. 'I will set out and go back to my father'" (Luke 15:18).

Amos told the Israelites there was no exit from God's judgment, but they continued to say, "Hurry up and end your sermon!" There was clear reason for the judgment of God and it was found in the twin sisters of Amos: social injustice and shallow religion.

Amos 8:4 says, *Hear this, you who trample on the needy and bring the poor of the land to an end.* That is Amos' resounding general indictment. The urban affluence had been built upon a disregard of the disadvantaged. Those, who at one time had been slaves themselves, became affluent and put their feet on the necks of others, were to become slaves once again.

This was the indictment of Amos to those who said of that generation, "Hurry up with the benediction." There is nothing wrong with affluence. If you hear Amos saying that affluence is bad, then you do not hear his message. Amos does not say affluence is bad; he says affluence is dangerous. It is a matter that is spiritually precarious.

At the zenith of the power of ancient Sparta, the city state in the Greek Peloponnesus, the Spartans sent to the oracle at Delphi and asked the priest who was there to give an oracle, "What can hurt the Spartans?" The oracle said, "Only the prosperity of the Spartans will make the Spartans vulnerable."[lxxxviii]

Amos spoke to a generation under the judgment of God with an affluence that in and of itself was not sin, but had become a transgression because it was built upon heaping indignities and injustices upon the disadvantaged who always, in the Old Testament, were the objects of Yahweh's special care.

What about the vision? Well, I said that Amos was given x-ray vision to get inside the heads of the worshipers. While they were not talking about suits, and hair styles, etc., they were talking about something else.

Amos quotes them in verse 5a. Sitting there with their eyes darting, their feet fidgeting, their thumbs twirling, and their minds calculating. *When will the new moon be over.*... During the hour of worship, what fills their minds? Their illegal schemes.

Amos 5b says, *that we may sell grain? And the Sabbath, that we may offer wheat for sale, that we may make the ephah small and the shekel great and deal deceitfully with false balances.* They're asking how they can make the ephah small. The ephah was a measure of volume, about 18 gallons, with which wheat was measured. They were calculating how they could rip people off from what was theirs. So, they occupy their hour of worship.

They also ask how to make the shekel great. They not only robbed via volume, but also robbed via currency. They asked how they could rip people off both coming and going.

As if that were not enough, they began asking if they could "deal deceitfully with false balances." Then, to make their scheming even worse during the worship service, they asked in verse 6, *that we may buy the poor for silver and the needy for a pair of sandals and sell the chaff of the wheat?* Not only will we sell it at deceitful volume and deceitful weight, but how can we take the wheat that has been trampled into the ground until there is no kernel left? Then, we can pawn off the poorest wheat on the poorest of people. This is how they occupied themselves during the hour of worship.

Amos probes their society deeply and sees their religious shallowness evidences of social injustice. There is an odd and peculiar statement in the Pentateuch. Exodus 20:2 says, *I am the* LORD *your God, who brought you out of the land of Egypt, out of the house of slavery.* God brought them out of Egypt and they went into places of worship to figure out how they could develop scams instead of worship God. Redemption and ethics must go together, but that was not so for the Israelites.

What is the reaction of God who listens to these fidgety false worshipers thinking "Hurry up with the benediction"? It is His oath in verse 7: *The* LORD *has sworn by the pride of Jacob: 'Surely I will never forget any of their deeds.'* This is a word of sarcasm. You swear by that which will not change. Jehovah found something that didn't seem to be changing: the arrogant pride of affluent Israel.

It has become so certain that He swears by it. Three times in this book, Jehovah takes an oath concerning the destiny of His people. We tend to think historically that northern Israel came to an end in 722 B.C. because of Tiglath Pilesar, or because of Sargon, or because of Shalmaneser, or other Assyrians, but that's not when Israel came to an end.[lxxxix] They came to an end when, by the oath of God, "TERMINAL" was written over that generation.

We better hear the Word of God in days of national debt to the tune of $21.1 Trillion.[xc] You see, our national destiny does not rest in whether Donald Trump or Mike Pence are effective leaders. Neither does it rest with what our country's primary business leaders do to keep jobs here in the USA. Our country's national destiny rests with the oath of God.

If God swears our nation will endure, then we will, but if God swears we will not endure due to national arrogance, try as we will, glory will have departed.

II. The Result of God's Judgment

The result is initially seen in a great reversal. In verses 8–10, Amos paints a scenario of everything in an affluent society, but overnight that is reversed.

> Amos 8:8–10 says, [8] *Shall not the land tremble on this account, and everyone mourn who dwells in it, and all of it rise like the Nile, and be tossed about and sink again, like the Nile of Egypt?* [9] *"And on that day," declares the Lord GOD, "I will make the sun go down at noon and darken the earth in broad daylight.* [10] *I will turn your feasts into mourning and all*

your songs into lamentation; I will bring sackcloth on every waist and baldness on every head; I will make it like the mourning for an only son and the end of it like a bitter day.

The end of verse 9 speaks of darkness hitting the earth. Astronomers tell us in 763 B.C., there was an eclipse of the sun.[xci] Perhaps this was considered a word from God against an errant generation.

Amos warns the generation of northern Israel in the 7th century B.C., and He warns us today that the God of Israel and the God of time and space is the God who can bring immediate reversal when His judgment comes. Light to darkness. Songs to dirges. Life to death.

There is an even more profound result when we say "Hurry up with the benediction." That result is that God gives us what we most want.

Verse 11 says, *Behold, the days are coming," declares the Lord GOD, 'when I will send a famine on the land—not a famine of bread, nor a thirst for water, but of hearing the words of the LORD.'* Two times in our prophecy, Amos' listeners said, "Shut up." In chapter 2, the crowd tells him "be gone!" In chapter 7, Amaziah, the king's preacher, tells him to go home. The judgment of God to a generation who says "Hurry up with the benediction" is to give them just what they want. There will be a famine—not for bread and water—but for the Word of God.

The most devastating judgments that God gives are not when God does something, but when He doesn't do something. It is not so much His presence as it is the awful silence of His absence.

Like King Midas, Amos' generation got what they wanted. They found that to touch it was a costly thing. They reversed the Lord's beatitude when He said, *Blessed are those who hunger and thirst for righteousness, for they shall be satisfied* (Matthew 5:6). To Amos, it could have said, "Cursed are those who have no hunger for the Word of God, for they shall get what they want and shall be famished."

Amos pictures them in verse 12 as finally they look for a word from God. *They shall wander from sea to sea, and from north to east; they shall run to and fro, to seek the word of the LORD, but they shall not find it.*

Oh, but a man's reach should exceed his grasp, and they reach out for a word from God, and like a shadow before them, they cannot catch it. They go from the Mediterranean to the Dead Sea. In verse 14, they go from Dan in the north to Beersheba in the south. They make a circuit, tottering like intoxicated men. They grope like blind men and stumble like ancient men. They're not looking for bread and water, but for a Word from God.

They finally find that in the generation that says to God's messenger, "Go home!," got what they wanted—no Word from the Lord. Even the strongest among them and the most beautiful were stricken with this judgment. Verse 13 says, *In that day the lovely virgins and the young men shall faint for thirst.* Are you in a hurry to get out of this worship serve to do something ungodly? Are you waiting for the benediction? Are you chomping at the bit for Monday to come?

Sometimes, we may say, "God, be gone. I don't want that Word." And God honors it. But then, a time of tragedy comes, or maybe it's a time of sickness, or grief, or loneliness. And we want a word from God, but we find that He honored our wish.

Conclusion

Amos did not know that that rejected word of God would one day become flesh in Bethlehem's manger. What Amos' terminal generation could not find, despised shepherds and traveling kings would discover that God's word had become flesh in that manger. As 1 Corinthians 2:9 says, *What no eye has seen, nor ear heard, nor the heart of man imagined, what God has prepared for those who love him."* God's word came and said in Matthew 4:4, *"Man shall not live by bread alone, but by every word that comes from the mouth of God.*

Two things ring out from this awful chapter of judgment. There is, in verse 3, that word "hush," "silence." There is in verse 9 that eclipse—darkness. Judgment of God to a generation that is thoroughly secular in silence and darkness.

But my mind takes me somewhere else, to a hillside outside of Jerusalem, where at noonday, there was a darkness worse than any eclipse. This is where the Son of God cried out, *My God, why have you forsaken me?* (Matthew 27:46) There was a silence, and the Son of God died in the hush of silence, and the darkness from judgment.

Thank God we're not left only with a word from Amos. We're left with that final Word of God on Calvary, dying in the hush of silence, in the darkness of judgment, that no generation may be the terminal generation.

May we be a people who wait on God's benediction rather than hurry to Monday.

9 | WHEN LIFE IS DESTROYED, IT CAN BE RESTORED

Amos 9

For eight chapters, we have heard the roar from the lion of Zion. We have stood with Amos through earthquake times. However, in this concluding chapter of studying the minor prophet book of Amos, the lion will no longer roar. The lion will lie down with the lamb. The lion will eat straw like an ox.

The title of this chapter is, "When Life is Destroyed, it Can be Restored." I am specifically talking about the fact that you have messed up, you will mess up, and God can put your broken life back together.

In the final word from Amos, judgment that is total becomes hope that is ultimate. The ninth chapter of Amos' prophecy ends with the most withering announcement of judgment to be found in the entirety of Amos' corpus, the literary residue that we have out from among his spoken words, and yet, at the same time, it has in it at its very end, among the most soaring aspirations that we find in any of the Hebrew prophets, the change in scenery from gloom and doom to the highest goodness has led some to say another hand is painting here on Amos' pallet. Someone else picked up the brush that Amos was using, perhaps 200-300 years later, and added to the picture of doom that Amos had painted with bright pastels of hope. And yet, must we must decide that the prophets of Hebrews only had to speak words of doom and gloom?

HOSEA

Hosea spoke words of doom to a generation that was known by Amos, and yet, out of the brokenness of Hosea's own home, he saw the hope of Jehovah become wed again, in purity and chastity, to his people. Hosea knew the tension of a proclamation of judgment and an announcement of hope.

ISAIAH

Wasn't Isaiah a prophet of both doom and hope? Calling down the judgment of God as the statesman prophet walked in the halls of government. And yet, naming one of his children "Shear-jashub," "a remnant shall return" (Isaiah 7:3). This was hope in the midst of doom.

JEREMIAH

Wasn't Jeremiah a prophet who walked in tension between doom and hope? Remember the field of Hananiah (Jer 28:10)? When Jeremiah had announced the withering and blistering judgment of Nebuchadnezzar's Babylon with a sealed deed and an opened deed, he bought a plot of ground in the very land that he had pronounced condemned. Like the Patrician Senator of Rome who bought at full market price the property where the armies of the Carthaginian Hannibal were kept, even so, Jeremiah, symbolically, acted out that morality play of hope.[xcii]

We must not say that the prophets of the Old Testament could not at the same time walk in the narrow, confining gorge and precipice of doom, and yet take the wanes of the morning and see times of hope. Who is this God of the prophets who holds us in tension between judgment and hope?

I. There is No Way to Escape God's Judgment

Amos 9:1 says, *I saw the Lord standing beside the altar, and he said: "Strike the capitals until the thresholds shake, and shatter them on the heads of all the people; and those who are left of them I will kill with the sword; not one of them shall flee away; not one of them shall escape.'*

Four times, in chapters 7 and 8, we've entered into the autobiography of Amos, gone aside into the hidden place at the genesis of his ministry. This is where visions from Jehovah filled both his waking and sleeping moments. The first of these judgments told us that judgment was on the way. Do you remember the vision of locusts and the vision of judgment by fire? In that first couplet of visions, Amos pleads in intercession, "Please, Lord. Cease!" The Lord hears that intercession and withholds the judgment that was coming.

However, then the plumb line falls to test the perpendicularity of Jacob. Then, Amos sees that ripened summer fruit. The very ripeness of which is the irreversible condition. That vision reminds Amos that Israel is beyond the time of intercession. Amos has clearly seen the fact that judgment is coming.

In chapter 9, we have the last and capstone vision, the concluding vision of Amos' autobiographical records. Now, he not only sees *that* judgment is coming, he also sees *how* it is coming. This vision differs from the other. Here, there is no intermediate revelatory object. He sees no locusts, no fire, no plumb line, no basket of ripened summer fruit. Here, he looks, and without any change of dialogue as we have seen before, stunned into silence by the verdict of God. He sees none other than the living God Himself standing, of all places, on the brazen altar in the outer court of the temple. This is without precedent anywhere in the Old Testament.

Amos had no precedent for this vision to see in superhuman, heroic dimensions the living God of Israel standing on the altar of burnt sacrifice. He was standing in that very place where that generation thought and supposed their worship placated Him and appeased Him. Standing there, not in appeasement, but ready to judge in a striking way. What does God do standing in the national cathedral at Bethel? Amos looks, and with his bare hand, minus any implement, he strikes out at the capitol of the columns of the door, and the building reverberates.

We're told in the Hebrew that the very thresholds shook.[xciii] The records we have indicate that those thresholds were somewhere around six to nine cubits deep in solid stone. Amos means to tell us in this capstone climactic vision that when God strikes at the house, it becomes the epicenter of an earthquake that sends out its reverberations over all of the land.

What is the consequence of this? The end of verse 1 says, *not one of them shall flee away; not one of them shall escape.*

In a fourfold, quadrupled, no-exit statement, Amos presses onto us about the God before whom we can stand in judgment and from whom there is no escape. God says He will . . .

(1) wound them in the head;

(2) sleigh the last of them with a sword;

(3) if there were one man who felt as if he were fleet enough by foot to escape the presence of the God of judgment, he will not escape away;

(4) lastly, even those who are taken captive by those leading away trains of exiles will not escape.

There is a warning here from Amos of the totality of judgment that awaited his generation. I wonder if you could share with me an experience that you had from which there is the futility of no escape.

As I combed back over my mind and life's experiences, I could think of some experiences from driving through the cumbersome traffic of my home city of Dallas. The cornucopia of cars whizzing by at God-forsaken speeds one moment, then being stuck for hours at a time in other moments created some unique times of life. I have one friend who was driving on those clogged freeways to Southwestern Seminary and a teenage boy was walking on the road, and my friend accidentally hit that boy and killed him. He was in a situation where he could not avoid that boy. There was no possible escape. To veer to the left, was to go into oncoming traffic at 70 MPH, and to go to the right was to drive over a bridge's lip. There was no escape . . . only waiting to see what would happen.

Amos wished to paint that picture for a generation over which there was written the words, "No exit." And, if they would dispute with him, he would draw the picture even more clearly.

He makes a fanciful attempt to describe God's sovereignty on the cosmic plane.

Amos 9:2 says, *If they dig into Sheol, from there shall my hand take them; if they climb up to heaven, from there I will bring them down.*

Amos imagines one who avoided all of God's efforts to shut him in, and he has dug through that barrier between the land of the living and Sheol (the land of the shades). Sheol was the grey and departed land spoken of in the Old Testament that often represented Hell. Perhaps this would-be fugitive does not think that God's sovereignty would extend into Sheol.[xciv]

But what does Amos say? "from there shall my hand take them." The hand of God means His capability and His effectiveness.[xcv] Amos knew what it meant to be taken by God. That is the very word used when he described how he was a shepherd and God took him.

There will be no fleeing to the realm of night, nor will there be flight to go to the heavens. Yahweh says that from there, he will be brought down. He is not the regional god of the Middle East, He is the God of the universe.

Then, God speaks to another fugitive. Amos 9:3 says, *If they hide themselves on the top of Carmel, from there I will search them out and take them;*

and if they hide from my sight at the bottom of the sea, there I will command the serpent, and it shall bite them.

I suppose if you were going to run away anywhere in Amos' end of the world, Carmel was the place to go. It was 500 meters high. It was covered with dense underbrush. It's the same word (יְתְבָּאוּ) that was used of Adam when he was hiding in the Garden of Eden.[xcvi] It is as if the whole world had become an Adam and an Eden.

There may have been a presupposition that Mount Carmel, because it was in a Baal worshiping district, was beyond the sovereignty of the Living God, and that a fugitive there would move beyond the pale of the hegemony of the God of Israel. Amos says "no." Even there, He will seek him and find him.

Verse 3b says that, *if they hide from my sight at the bottom of the sea, there I will command the serpent, and it shall bite them.* The chaotic sea, which has always been at enmity with God, even the sea serpent, whom according to both Job and the Psalmist, God has barely (if it all) tamed.[xcvii] The enemy of God will become His ally in seeking that fugitive.

Oh, how Amos could close every door on his generation to impress them that there was no escape from the judgment that was coming.

Finally, Amos imagines them in a concrete, historical situation.

Amos 9:4a says, *And if they go into captivity before their enemies, there I will command the sword, and it shall kill them.*

Amos imagines a day when even their enemies, the blood curdling Assyrians, will look like their Saviors in comparison to a meeting with the living God. I think I hear the words of the author of Hebrews. It is a fearful thing to fall into the hands of a living God. Amos explains that even captivity will seem like escape if it means not a head-on collision with the Living God of Israel.

Then, at the end of verse 9, God gives the final blow: *and I will fix my eyes upon them for evil and not for good.*

This slave nation of Israelites has known what it was like for God to transfix their enemies with His gaze. This is precisely the phrase that is used of the Living God where he used His eye to freeze Pharaoh and the army during the exodus.[xcviii] However, now that power that had been leveraged on behalf of the covenant people will become operative against them.

Application

How does this word from Amos apply to us 2,800 years later? It teaches us that, if nothing else, there are many worse things than meeting your political enemies. In these days of political ads, mounting unemployment numbers, increasing national and average personal debt, military presence in Iraq and Afghanistan, and whether or not we are seeing the insipient days of battle with the North Koreans. We must remember from the word of Amos that there is something worse than meeting our political enemies, and that is meeting the Living God if we are under His judgment.

We noted in the previous chapter that the oath of God is that which can protect us or deliver us, and we leave everything in His hands. That is the significant thing.

II. Everyone Stands On Level Ground Before God

One could guess that Amos' auditors at the national cathedral said that they don't particularly care for preaching like that. So they began to take issue with his scheme for total judgment of Israel. One can almost hear them: "Well, we are the people of the covenant. We have a manifest destiny. We're all God's got. He's got to preserve us." And Amos answers them in such a way that was unexpected and striking. Amos tells the Israelites there is ultimately nothing unique about them. He is the God of the exodus people, but he is the God of many an exodus. And He is the God of all nations as the author and consummator of their history.

Look at Amos 9:7. He was saying this to a proud and arrogant group of people who felt like they had God in a box with reference to their own future. Amos warns them by saying, *'Are you not like the Cushites to me, O people of Israel?' declares the* LORD.

The Cushites were the inhabitants of the interior of Africa.[xcix] They're from down below the second cataract of the Nile where it makes its great "S" shape.[c] To the Hebrew of Samaria, it would have been considered the most remote corner of the earth.[ci] God levels them by saying that they are on the same ground as the people who live way out in the middle of nowhere. God was explaining that there is not a uniqueness of Israel that would insulate them from judgment.

Here is the first time, in all of the prophetic books, a note of universalism hitherto unseen in all of the Old Testament. He was saying that He is the God of all people, even the most remote people you can imagine.

The Israelites talk back to their preacher and say, "Ah, but we're the people of the exodus, Amos." Well, God has a surprising word for them at just that point. He is the God who has led many an exodus. The end of verse 7 says, *Did I not bring up Israel from the land of Egypt, and the Philistines from Caphtor and the Syrians from Kir?*

That was the cruelest blow of all. The Philistines and the Aramians were ancient enemies of God's people. Only King David had finally subjugated the Philistines. Now, Amos tells them that God is not only the author of the history of all of Israel, but He is also the author of the history of their bitterest enemies. He not only led an exodus for the Israelites out of Egypt, but He also led an exodus for the Philistines, and eventually led them to be destroyed by King David.

He led the Syrians out of the Arabic stepland, and He disposed of them under Jeroboam. God, who disposed of them, waits (if necessary) to dispose of you.

Oh, what a withering word it was to hear that the God whom they thought they had in a box was the God who was responsible for the authorship and the disposition of their natural enemies.

Application

How does this word of Amos apply to us?

NATIONALLY

Church, in so many ways, it applies to us nationally. As I have stated many times in this book, America is not the covenant people of God. Americans are not God's covenant people. We are a country who impresses upon our currency, "In God we trust."

But this message from Amos, do not presume on any manifest destiny from God comes to us. And it reminds us just as much that God is the author of the creation of the third world nation in the deepest interior of the a backward continent as He is of our history. God can gather for Himself a people from anywhere.

INDIVIDUALLY

This is also a word for each of us individually. Would there be a person reading this who, with so much arrogance, hubris, and pride, that you feel the kingdom of God rests upon your shoulders? And to presume that you have such a prestigious place in His puzzle that, do what you may, He has got to have you?

The word of Amos is that the God of the history of all peoples is yours and mine. He can make Himself a new one any day He has to do so.

III. God Has A Bright and Hopeful Future for You

Suddenly, without explanation, Amos' symphony moves from the minor key to major chords. Suddenly, He stops painting with the drab greys and begins to paint with bright pastels.

Some theologians are so smitten with the difference that they say everything Amos said before was blood and iron, and now we have lavender and roses.[cii] They claim Amos couldn't have written that. Could this be true? Is it true that Amos did not write the latter portion of chapter 9?

The words of hope that Amos uses take the wings of the morning and soar beyond any expectation before him.

Global Reign of God with a Descendant of David

Amos 9:11 says, *In that day I will raise up the booth of David that is fallen and repair its breaches, and raise up its ruins and rebuild it as in the days of old,*

Amos' mind races ahead of him into what, even to him, must have been centuries. And he sees there the city of David fallen. The state of Judah was crushed into the dust. The empire of David had vanished. The throne of David had become like a miserable booth. Amos imagines Israel falling to such a lower degree, and then out of that, a global reign of the living God through one of the descendants of David.

One has to wait until that throne of David has becomes Bethlehem's manger. It was in the city of David, where out of that hopelessness, Amos' prophecy found fulfillment. That is the first article of Amos' hope.

Man will be Redeemed with His Environment

Amos 9:13 says, *'Behold, the days are coming,' declares the LORD, 'when the plowman shall overtake the reaper and the treader of grapes him who sows the seed; the mountains shall drip sweet wine, and all the hills shall flow with it.'*

You must understand that biblically, political redemption is not so much "rescue out of" as "redemption in the midst of." It has always been the intention of the biblical God to redeem man in man's environment. What Amos mentions here is a reversal of the curse of Genesis 3.

It is the theology of the Old Testament that man's environment has come to reflect the futility of man's spiritual life. When Amos' day of hope finally becomes sight and reality, the futility of the curse will be reversed.

In Palestine, people plow in late fall and reap in late spring.[ciii] The treading out of the grapes takes place in September. The planting of the seeds in the vineyards occurs in December.[civ] Amos envisions a day when, behind the man who is breaking the ground, there will come the reaper who is saying "move over." And behind the one who is treading up the grapes will be a man saying, "hurry up."

Amos shares that vision that the Apostle Paul catches in Romans 8:22, *For we know that the whole creation has been groaning together in the pains of childbirth until now.* Creation is groaning and waiting for redemption! If there is anything certain about the biblical message of redemption, it is that if God intends to redeem our souls, He intends to redeem our environment where Christ will reign. We worship a God who will redeem both man and man's environment.

He will remove the futility of life. Amos 9:14 says, *I will restore the fortunes of my people Israel, and they shall rebuild the ruined cities and inhabit them; they shall plant vineyards and drink their wine, and they shall make gardens and eat their fruit.*

If you have been in tune with this study of Amos, you may remember that in the fifth chapter, Amos said that the judgment of God meant that they will build stone houses, but never live in them. They would plant vineyards, but never drink from them. They would sow their gardens, but never eat from them.

Now, in this crescendo of hope, Amos sees that the futility of life will be reversed in that day when men and women will successfully live in what they have built. They will drink from the vines they have planted. They will eat from the fruit of their hands. A life of futility will be a thing of the past.

Man will be redeemed in his environment. This means there will be an equal and just distribution. In a world where the rich no longer have everything and the poor have nothing, that which Amos has mentioned again and again, will be gone forever in God's coming day when Christ shall reign.

Well, how does this happen? Where is the big revival meeting? When did their minds change? When was there an altar call? What is amazing is that after nine chapters of gloom and doom, Amos says nothing about the repentance of man that leads to this. It is all the radical initiative of God.

God says that He will raise up the tabernacle. He will raise up the ruins. He will build up as in the days of old.

The drowning man who clings for a life preserver when he tells the story does not amplify himself for reaching out for that which saves him; he speaks of the one who threw it. And so Amos, when speaking of God's last gracious coming reign, speaks not of the response of men, but of the initiative of God who makes it possible.

Is this accurate with what we know of the New Testament revelation of our Lord? Man redeemed in his environment? Let me call your mind to the last pictures of the book of Revelation. The new Jerusalem comes down out of Heaven. The Living God is not saying He will snatch people up out of any environment people have ever known to take them away to another day.

Amos concludes his minor prophet book with good news. In a world of increasing military tension and real estate frustration, it is comforting to know that not only will God redeem man, but also the environment of man. He will reverse the Genesis 3 curse.

He is the God whose judgment cannot be escaped, but He is also the God whose future is hope.

Dr. Jeremy Roberts

ABOUT THE AUTHOR | DR. JEREMY ROBERTS

Dr. Jeremy Roberts is Lead Pastor of Brushy Creek Baptist Church, Taylors, SC (suburban Greenville). This historic congregation is known as the "Mother Church of Greenville," and has faithfully reached Upstate South Carolina since George Washington's presidency. Dr. Roberts has preached on five continents, speaking at conferences, teaching at theological institutions, and advising political leaders, particularly on the topic of the intermingling of religion, millennials, and technology.

Roberts serves as an adjunct professor at Midwestern Baptist Theological Seminary and Liberty University, where he earned his D.Min. He blogs and podcasts regularly at JeremyRoberts.org and lives with his wife, Charity, and their two daughters, Autumn and Lily in the Greenville area.

Connect with Dr. Roberts online:

Twitter/Instagram: @JeremyPRoberts
Facebook.com/DrJeremyRoberts
Blog: JeremyRoberts.org
Brushy Creek Baptist Church, Taylors, SC: BrushyCreek.org

---

i Flyer Staff, "Another Oklahoma Earthquake Felt in Northwest Arkansas," *Fayetteville Flyer* (Nov 7, 2011); accessed online at http://www.fayettevilleflyer.com/2011/11/07/another-oklahoma-earthquake-felt-in-northwest-arkansas/.

ii James Ussher, *The Annals of the World* (Green Forest, AR: Master Books, 2003), 896.

iii Billy Smith and Frank S. Page, *NAC* Vol. *Vol. 19B: Amos, Obadiah, Jonah* (Nashville: Broadman & Holman Publishers, 2001), 37. Tekoa probably is the Judahite village about ten miles south of Jerusalem, not the Galilean Tekoa mentioned in the Talmud. Joab brought a wise woman from Tekoa to convince David to allow his son Absalom to return to the court (2 Sam 14:1–24). The village supplied one of David's mighty men (2 Sam 23:26). Rehoboam fortified it to defend his kingdom (2 Chr 11:5–12). Tekoa must have been a suitable site for breeding and tending sheep.

iv St. Jerome, ed. Walter J. Burghardt, *The Letters of St. Jerome* (Mahwah, NJ: Paulist Press, 1963), 67.

v Carl G. Rasmussen, *Zondervan Atlas of the Bible* (Grand Rapids: Zondervan, 2010), 49. Rasmussen describes in great detail the terrain of Tekoa. Interestingly, its location on the edge of the desert gave Amos an abnormally clear perspective of various cultures within a 15-mile radius.

vi Tod Linafelt, Timothy Beal, and Claudia V. Camp, *The Fate of King David: The Pasto and Present of a Biblical Icon* (New York: T&T Clark International, 2010), 127.

vii William Smith, *Dictionary of the Bible* (Cambridge, MA: Riverside Press, 1897), 2,990.

viii Pierre Berton, *The Comfortable Pew: A Critical Look at Christianity and the Religious Establishment in the New Age* (Philadelphia: Lippincott, 1965).

ix More details needed.

x Smith and Page, 37.

xi *The Pulpit Commentary: Amos.* 2004 (H. D. M. Spence-Jones, Ed.) (43). Bellingham, WA: Logos Research Systems, Inc.

xii D. N. Freedman, A. C. Myers, and A. B. Beck. *Eerdmans Dictionary of the Bible* (Grand Rapids: Eerdmans, 2000) 1,350. Uzziah's years were marked with relative peace and prosperity.

xiii Ibid.

xiv S. J. Schultz and G. V. Smith, *Exploring the Old Testament* (Wheaton: Crossway Books, 2001), 78. In religious matters Jeroboam took the initiative in leading his people astray. Fearing that the people might be diverted in their political loyalty by going to Jerusalem to worship, Jeroboam instituted idolatry by erecting golden calves at Bethel and Dan. Ignoring Mosaic restrictions, he appointed priests and allowed the Israelites to offer sacrifices at high places throughout the land. Jeroboam even officiated at the altar and changed feast days (cf. 1 Kings 12:25–33).

xv A. Negev, *The Archaeological encyclopedia of the Holy Land*, 3rd ed. (New York: Prentice Hall Press, 1990).

xvi John Phillips, *Bible Explorer's Guide: How to Understand and Interpret the Bible* (Grand Rapids: Kregel, 1987), 137. Phillips explains in great detail the importance of the number three. Here are some examples he notes: It takes three lines to enclose a space and draw a geometric figure. It takes three dimensions to make a solid, three persons in grammar to express and include all of mankind's relationships, three divisions to express time, three kingdoms to sum up things that exist (animal, vegetable, mineral), three forms to complete the sum of human capability (thought, word, deed). Three is evidently an important number. God Himself is in three persons (Father, Son, Holy Spirit). The holy of holies was a perfect cube, ten by ten by ten cubits. Christ has three offices: Prophet, Priest, and King. Jesus' resurrection took place on the third day.

xvii Billy Smith and Frank S. Page, *NAC* Vol. *Vol. 19B: Amos, Obadiah, Jonah* (Nashville: Broadman & Holman Publishers, 2001), 47. The term may be translated "transgressions," "rebellions," "crimes," or "sins." The wrongdoing named in each oracle represented rebellion against God's standard of conduct, not simply rebellion against Judah or Israel based on prior treaty agreements. With the sin named, Damascus had exceeded the limit of God's tolerance.

xviii Christa Salamandra, *A New Old Damascus: Authenticity and Distinction in Urban Syria* (Bloomington, IN: Indiana University Press, 2004), 27.

xix James Hastings, ed., *Encyclopaedia of Religion and Ethics*, Vol. VIII, (Edinburgh: T&T Clark, 1916), 899.

xx For an historic perspective of Alsace-Lorraine, see Coleman Phillipson, *Alsace-Lorraine: Past, Present, and Future* (London: T.F. Unwin, Ltd., 1918).

xxi Smith and Page, 48. Use of sledges with iron spikes driven through them increased the efficiency of threshing. Such an implement drawn over helpless captives, if taken literally, brings to mind shamelessly brutal conduct.

xxii Waard, J. d., Smalley, W. A., & Smalley, W. A. (1979). *A translator's handbook on the book of Amos*. Helps for translators (33). Stuttgart: United Bible Societies.

xxiii Jerome Murphy, *Oxford Archaeological Guides: The Holy Land* (Oxford: Oxford University Press, 2008), 14–15.

xxiv Ibid.

xxv J. Andrew Dearman and M. Patrick Graham, eds., *The Land That I Will Show You: Essays on the History and Archaeology of the Ancient Near East* (Sheffield, England: Sheffield University Press, 2001), 147.

xxvi Philip J. King, *Amos, Hosea, Micah: An Archaeological Commentary* (Philadelphia: Westminster Press, 1988), 50.

xxvii Susan Pollock, *Ancient Mesopotamia* (Cambridge, England: Cambridge University Press, 1999), 21.

xxviii Victor H. Matthews and Don C. Benjamin, *Old Testament Parallels: Laws and Stories from the Ancient Near East*, 3rd ed. (Mahwah, NJ: Paulis Press, 2006), 182.

xxix Ibid.

xxx J. Elliott Corbitt, *Prophets on Main Street* (Louisville: John Knox Press, 1978).

xxxi Robert Morkot, *Historical Dictionary of Ancient Egyptian Warfare* (Lanham, MD: The Rowman and Littlefield Publishing Group, 2003), xxi.
xxxii Barbara Kadden and Bruce Kadden, *Teaching Mitzvot: Concepts, Values, and Activities* (Denver: A. R. E. Publishing, 2003), 11.

xxxiii Billy Smith and Frank S. Page, *NAC Vol. 19B: Amos, Obadiah, Jonah* (Nashville: Broadman & Holman Publishers, 2001), 70.

xxxiv Peter C. Craigie, *Twelve Prophets: Hosea, Joel, Amos, Obadiah, and Jonah* (Louisville: John Knox Press, 1984), 149.

xxxv The divide between Israelites and Egyptians may be further explored in Alexandra Nocke, *The Place of the Mediterranean in Modern Israeli Identity* (The Netherlands: Brill, 2009), 208ff.

xxxvi M. Bentley, *Opening up Amos* (Leominster: Day One Publications, 2006), 43.

xxxvii Smith and Page, 71.

xxxviii Nora Tai-Xiu Groves, "Our Trip to China," *LA Times* (Dec 15, 2004); accessed online at http://www.latimes.com/news/la-chinatrip-nora-story,0,4673945.story.

xxxix William Henry Hudson, *A Shepherd's Life: Impressions of the South Wiltshire Downs* (New York: Cambridge University Press, 2010), 145.

xl For a more in-depth study of the spiritual gift of prophecy, see Wayne A. Grudem, *The Gift of Prophecy in the New Testament and Today* (Wheaton: Crossway Books, 2000).
xli Thomas E. Levy, *The Archaeology of Society in the Holy Land* (New York: Leicester University Press, 1998), 394–95.

xlii This famous sermon was preached a multitude of places including Highland Park Baptist Church, Chattanooga, TN. This is mentioned in the biography of Dr. Lee Roberson. James H. Wigton, *Lee Roberson: Always About His Father's Business* (Maitland, FL: Xulon Press, 2010), 241.

xliii Sarah Bradford, *Lucrezia Borgia: Life, Love, and Death in Renaissance Italy* (London: Penguin Books, 2005).

xliv Cecil Blanche Fitzgerald Woodham-Smith, *Florence Nightingale: 1820–1910* (London: Constable, 1996).

xlv Duane W. Roller, *Cleopatra: A Biography* (Oxford: Oxford University Press, 2010). Angela Leighton, *Victorian Women Poets: Writing Against the Heart* (Charlottesville: University of Virginia Press, 1992).

xlvi Billy Smith and Frank S. Page, *NAC Vol. 19B: Amos, Obadiah, Jonah* (Nashville: Broadman & Holman Publishers, 2001), 24.

xlvii Ibid., 93–94.

xlviii Ibid.

xlix Robert K. Brown and Mark R. Norton, *The One Year Songs of Faith* (Carol Stream, IL: Tyndale House Publishers, 1995), 37.

l

li *Time*, May 25, 1987.

lii As Kennedy points out, "A disturbing book that shows the depth of immorality in America is *The Day America Told the Truth: What People Really Believe About Everything That Really Matters,* by James Patterson and Peter Kim (New York: Prentice Hall, 1991). They conclude: 'In effect, we're all making up our own moral codes' (p. 6). Another recommended book on America's immorality points to the correct way back, though Christianity. It's by Harry and Betty Dent and is entitled, *Right vs. Wrong: Solutions to the American Nightmare* (Nashville: Thomas Nelson Publishers, 1992)."

liii D. James Kennedy, *What if Jesus Had Never Been Born?* (Nashville: Thomas Nelson, 2001).

liv

lv

lvi Tyler Mason, "Minor League Saints Hosting Night for Atheists," *Fox Sports North* (July 12, 2012); accessed online at http://www.foxsportsnorth.com/07/12/12/Minor-league-Saints-hosting-night-for-at/msn_landing.html?blockID=759992&feedID=5930.

lvii Barry Alan Shain, *The Myth of American Individualism: The Protestant Origins of America* (Princeton, NJ: Princeton University Press, 1994), 193.

lviii Rufus Spain and Samuel S. Hill, *At Ease in Zion: Social History of Southern Baptists, 1865–1900* (Tuscaloosa, AL: University of Alabama Press, 2003).

lix F. Brown, S. R. Driver, and C. A. Briggs, *Enhanced Brown-Driver-Briggs Hebrew and English Lexicon* (Oak Harbor, WA: Logos Research Systems, 2000), 983. S. V., "שַׁאֲנָן".

lx Ibid., S. V., "בָּטַח".

lxi David Noel Freedman, *Eerdmans Dictionary of the Bible* (Grand Rapids: William B. Eerdmans Publishing Company, 2000), 211.

lxii Thomas Kelly Cheyne, *Traditions and Beliefs of Ancient Israel* (London: Adam and Charles Black, 1907), 153.

lxiii Ann E. Killebrew, *Biblical Principles and Ethnicity: An Archaeological Study of Egyptians, Canaanites, Philistines: Archaeology and Biblical Studies* (Leiden, The Netherlands: Brill, 2005), 14–20.

lxiv Jonathan Swift, *Gulliver's Travels* (Dover, DE: Dover Publications, 1996).

lxv Soren Kierkegaard, *Sickness Unto Death* (Radford, VA: A & D Publishing, 2008).

lxvi Thomas E. Levy and Thomas Higham, "The Bible and Radiocarbon Dating: Archaeology, Test and Science," *Equinox Publishing* (July 13, 2012); accessed online at http://haifa.academia.edu/NormaFranklin/Papers/170638/Correlation_and_Chronology_Samaria_and_Megiddo_Redux

lxvii Smith and Page, *NAC*, 118.

lxviii To learn more about Bacchanalian banquets, see Philip J. King and Lawrence E. Stager, *Life in Biblical Israel* (Louisville: John Knox Press, 2001), 355. Succinctly, these Greek smorgasbords would involve masses of food and orgies. Alcohol would typically flow in abundance at these gatherings. Cf. Jeremiah 16:5 to see the only other example of this in the Bible. These feasts lasted several days.

lxix To learn more about the nomadic and pastoral tendencies of the Hebrew people, see Craig A. Lockard, *Societies, Networks, and Transitions: To 600* (Boston: Wadsworth, 2011), 65.

lxx F. I. Andersen and D. N. Freedman, *Amos: A New Translation with Introduction and Commentary* (AB 24A; New York/London/Toronto: Doubleday, 1989), 562. cf. D. N. Freedman, "But Did King David Invent Musical Instruments?" *BRev* 1/2 (1985) 51.

lxxi Ibid.

lxxii Smith and Page, *NAC*, 118.

lxxiii Helmet Thieleke, *Encounter with Spurgeon* (Cambridge: James Clarke & Co., Ltd., 1964), 236.

lxxiv http://www.lasvegassun.com/news/2001/jun/25/payback-gaming-pioneer-redd-looks-back-on-a-lifeti/.

[lxxv] Tom Freiling, *Reagan's God and Country: A President's Moral Compass: His Beliefs on God, Religious Freedom, the Sanctity of Life and More* (Ventura, CA: Regal Books, 2000), 152.

[lxxvi] J. Daniel Hays and Tremper Longman III, *The Message of the Prophets: A Survey of the Prophetic and Apocalyptic Books of the Old Testament* (Grand Rapids: Zondervan, 2010), 278.

[lxxvii] John D. Whiting, "Jerusalem's Locust Plague," National Geographic (1915): 511–50, esp. p. 529, describes the locust plague of 1915 in Palestine and observes that the locusts gnawed off the small limbs of the fig trees, resembling "white candles on a dried up Christmas tree." George Adam Smith also details descriptively a swarm of locusts he personally saw in the Middle East, *The Book of the Twelve Prophets* (New York: Armstrong and Son, 1903), 398–99.

[lxxviii] For more info on panzer divisions, see Steve Kane, *The First SS Panzer Division in the Battle of the Bulge* (Bennington, VT: Merriam Press, 2008).

[lxxix] Warren W. Wiersbe, *The Wiersbe Commentary: The Complete Old Testament in One Volume* (Colorado Springs: David C. Cook Publishers, 2007), 1310.

[lxxx] Robert N. Bellah, *Habits of the Heart: Individualism and Commitment in American Life* (Berkeley: University of California Press, 1985), 201.

[lxxxi] J. Vernon McGee, *Genesis through Revelation* (Nashville: Thomas Nelson, 1998), ch. 7.

[lxxxii] F. Brown, S. R. Driver, and C. A. Briggs, *Enhanced Brown-Driver-Briggs Hebrew and English Lexicon* (Oak Harbor, WA: Logos Research Systems, 2000), 983. S. V., אֲדֹנָי יְהוִה.

[lxxxiii] Ibid., "אָמַר".

[lxxxiv] Hassell Bullock, *An Introduction to Old Testament Prophetic Books* (Chicago: Moody Press, 2007), 86.

[lxxxv] F. Brown, S. R. Driver, and C. A. Briggs, *Enhanced Brown-Driver-Briggs Hebrew and English Lexicon* (Oak Harbor, WA: Logos Research Systems, 2000), 983. S. V., "כְּלוּב קָיִץ".

[lxxxvi] Smith and Page, 143.

[lxxxvii] Max Lucado, *God's Story, Your Story: When His Becomes Yours* (Grand Rapids: Zondervan, 2011), 72.

lxxxviii H. Michell, *Sparta* (Cambridge: Cambridge University Press, 1964), 109.

lxxxix Edwin Richard Thiele, *The Mysterious Numbers of the Hebrew Kings* (Grand Rapids: Zondervan, 1983), 125.

xc "U. S. Debt Clock," *U. S. National Debt Clock: Real Time* (July 31, 2012); accessed online at http://www.usdebtclock.org/.

xci David H. Kelley and Eugene F. Milone, *Exploring Ancient Skies: A Survey of Ancient and Cultural Astronomy* (New York: Springer Press, 2011), 222.
xcii Andreas Kluth, *Hannibal and Me: What History's Greatest Military Strategist Can Teach Us About Success and Failure* (New York: Riverhead Books, 2011), 42.

xciii Smith and Page, 154. The remainder of the monologue magnifies the action of God. Some interpreters suggest an earthquake as the response to the Lord's command (the verb *rāʿaš* is from the same root as the noun for "earthquake" used in chapter 1).

xciv To learn more about Sheol, read Philip S. Johnston, *Shades of Sheol: Death and Afterlife in the Old Testament* (Downers Grove, IL: Intervarsity Press, 2002).

xcv Alistair Begg, *The Hand of God* (Grand Rapids: Zondervan, 1999).

xcvi F. Brown, S. R. Driver, and C. A. Briggs, *Enhanced Brown-Driver-Briggs Hebrew and English Lexicon* (Oak Harbor, WA: Logos Research Systems, 2000), S. V., "יְחָבְאוּ"

xcvii This reference to the sea serving as a symbol as chaos is clarified in John's writing of Revelation. Particularly, the beast in the sea in Revelation 13.

xcviii See Exodus 8 and 13.

xcix James Luther Mays, *Amos: A Commentary* (London: SCM Canterbury Press, 1969), 157.

c Christopher Ehret, *The Civilizations of Africa: A History to 1800* (Charlottesville, VA: University of Virginia Press, 2002), 121.

ci Mays, 157.

cii Jorg Jeremias, *The Book of Amos: A Commentary* (Louisville: John Knox Press, 1995), 162ff.

---

ciii Leland Ryken, James C. Wilhoit, and Tremper Longman III, *Dictionary of Biblical Imagery* (Downers Grove, IL: InterVarsity Press, 1998), 270.

civ Ibid.

95982343R00102

Made in the USA
Columbia, SC
27 May 2018